PROMOTIONAL STRATEGIES
for
BOOKS

HOW TO MARKET & PROMOTE YOUR BOOK

THE AMAZON SELF PUBLISHER SERIES, BOOK 2

DALE L. ROBERTS

Amazon Reviews for Books: How to Get Book Reviews on Amazon

By Dale L. Roberts

©2020 One Jacked Monkey, LLC

Amazon is a registered trademark of Amazon.com, Inc. This book is not authorized or endorsed by Amazon.com, Inc.

Twitter is a registered trademark of Twitter, Inc. This book is not authorized or endorsed by Twitter, Inc.

Google and the Google logo are registered trademarks of Google LLC, used with permission. However, Google does not endorse any of the statements in this publication.

Some recommended links in this book are part of affiliate programs. This means if you purchase a product through one of the links, then I get a portion of each sale. It doesn't affect your cost and greatly helps support the cause. If you have any reservations about buying a product through my affiliate link, then feel free to Google a direct link and bypass the affiliate link.

Cover design by MaMarko78 on Fiverr. To see his services, visit: https://dalelinks.com/coversbymarko.

Find out how I found Marko and why I selected him for cover design services in the video at https://dalelinks.com/5designs.

Interior design and typesetting by Archangel Ink at ArchangelInk.com.

ISBN: 978-1-950043-20-0

| Promotion ▾ | *Contents* | 🔍 |

*P*romotional Strategies for Books is the culmination of over six years in the self-publishing business and learning from the best in the industry. Since starting my YouTube channel, Self-Publishing with Dale, I learned my viewers wanted more from me than videos. Naturally, a person dispensing self-publishing advice should have books about the topic, right? Well, not in my case. For the better part of my self-publishing career, I wrote and published books about health and fitness, not self-publishing.

About one month ago, I finally pivoted away from fitness and into the world of self-publishing information. Between building the Self-Publishing with Dale brand, managing the books I published previously, and coaching self-publishers, I never made this content shift a priority.

Once I stopped making excuses and started taking action, I created the *Amazon Self-Publisher Series*. This short series of books focuses on the most common pain points of authors and self-publishers using the Amazon platform, including:

1. Keywords

2. Marketing and promotion

3. Reviews

Yes, you could skip reading this book and piece together all the content from my nearly 500 videos on YouTube. Maybe you could find your way through online articles, free courses, and expert interviews. The biggest issue you face is knowing what is right or wrong, current or outdated, and relevant or irrelevant.

What if you could get most everything you need to take action now? Imagine cutting through all the noise and getting the info to actively move the needle in your business.

Enter the *Amazon Self-Publisher Series*.

Promotional Strategies for Books: How to Market & Promote Your Book is the next logical step in this three-part series. In the first part, you learned how keywords can make or break discoverability on Amazon. Now, you're going to learn how to pour jet fuel on that fire, so you greatly increase your likelihood of discoverability. With these promotional strategies in your arsenal, you are at a greater advantage than other authors who publish and pray for the best.

I'm confident once you read through this three-part series, you'll handle the biggest issues plaguing most self-publishers using the Amazon platform. Let's get onto the next best step in your self-publishing journey. Enjoy and happy publishing!

–Dale L. Roberts

Rejection is a hard pill to swallow. To make matters worse, it was my eighteenth birthday. Usually, you'd think this was a monumental event. After all, it was the day I officially became a man. Everyone wants to share in this big day, and I was no different. This day teemed with errors and oversights. It all came down to me, who I knew, and how I made others aware of my birthday celebration.

Not to sound like a complete ingrate, I was thankful to spend my birthday with my mother. She was kind enough to be there for me on my big birthday and went out of her way to buy a half sheet of birthday cake and the essentials. My mother even drove half an hour out of her way to ring in my birthday. She was the only person to celebrate with me.

Being far away from home and having very few friends growing up did me no favors. The few people I knew from my hometown were merely one block away in another dormitory. I felt a certain kinship to them since we came from such a small town. I often questioned if this feeling was mutual and soon found out it wasn't.

All I had to do was invite people to my birthday, the place to meet (my dorm room), and get a general headcount. It seemed like I had everyone I knew on board, including the hometown acquaintances and a few new friends. I expected at least a dozen or more people. That's not too bad and was more than sufficient for an intimate celebration.

3

The time came, and my mother was already there with bells on. I waited for my friends to stop by and hang out with them. We could scarf down a tasty cake while chatting about our newfound college life.

That time never came. No one showed. Five minutes passed, and I figured they were simply on their way. Ten minutes passed, and I grew a bit concerned about their well-being. Fifteen minutes passed, and my mother began to think the half sheet might have been an overspend. Finally, I mustered up the nerve to call my expected attendees. A few of the phones remained unanswered. Once I finally got one person on the phone, I mentioned it was my birthday and wondered if he was still coming.

To my surprise, he wasn't aware of the celebration. Though, looking back, I don't believe there was any shock on his part. It was more how he tried to cover his tracks. The guy didn't want to come, but he wrangled the few stragglers from our hometown, and they slowly moseyed over to my dorm room. No sooner had my mother dished out their cake, they all inhaled it, said the obligatory "happy birthday," and left quicker than they came. Most of the cake remained intact, along with my shattered confidence, self-esteem, and emotions.

Keeping a brave face on, I thanked my mom for coming. When we parted ways, she left the large remaining portion of cake as a reminder of my failed attempt at my first birthday celebration in adulthood.

Launching a book is much the same way. As an author, you laboriously toil away at a manuscript. You've spent all your time, energy, attention, and money into this love of yours. It's remarkable, and why not? It's a piece of you that you want the world to share. It's a milestone all your friends, family, acquaintances, and even strangers should share in.

Yet, what do you do when no one shows to partake in your work? More specifically, how do you get more people to read your book? What do you need to do beyond writing that'll get people to buy and read your book?

What I conveniently didn't share with you in my story was the lack of preparation I had. Also, I didn't do a good enough job in communicating how important this celebration was. And, while my hometown buddies shared a little in common with me, they didn't share enough in common to make it worth their while to eat cake with someone they didn't feel particularly fond of. After all, college parties were more about keg stands and beer bongs, not sugary cake and fruit punch. I had a complete disconnect with my audience and failed to build awareness around the event.

The failed birthday party was on me, and so is a failed book on the author. If your book isn't doing well, it's on you. It's not on your audience. It's not on the platform that distributes it. The ultimate success of your publication relies solely on your ability to market and promote it. It doesn't just start days before the publication date. Marketing and promotion don't end once your launch date comes. They're unending tasks if you ever want to see consistent success in your publication.

Rather than writing and publishing your next book to an audience of crickets, you're going to learn how to solve that problem ASAP. There'll be no more pity parties for your book launch. Forget about making your mother the only recipient of your book. We're going to help troubleshoot your lack of book sales while offering up sensible and practical steps for marketing and promoting your book to the moon and back. With every launch, you'll get more and more people.

In due time, your audience will hit critical mass, and you'll look back on your previous missteps fondly like I do about my sad eighteenth birthday party. Let's dig into this tasty dessert known as *Promotional Strategies for Books*, and get you fast on your way to your book's greatest successes! The good news is you won't have to eat any extra calories or do any keg stands to get there. See you on the next page!

*Y*ou may have heard this phrase thrown around time and again, but do you truly know what marketing and promotion mean? Though each is mentioned one with the other, they both play a slightly different part. However, one doesn't function well without the other. If your marketing is off, then your promotional efforts won't amount to jack. And, if your promotional strategies suck, then your marketing will be all for naught.

Marketing boils down to the overall appearance, viability, and accessibility of your brand. It's how consumers (also known as the market) view you, your services, your product, and your overall brand. If you don't put any time or effort into who your audience and their expectations, your marketing sucks. However, if you get to know your ideal reader and their needs, then your marketing plan is bound to be off to a much better start.

Before you even publish your work, it's important to dial in for whom you are writing. Here are a few questions to consider:

1. Who is your ideal reader?

2. What is your ideal reader's problem?

3. What does your ideal reader expect from your book?

4. What has your ideal reader come to expect from your niche?

7

When considering these questions, track down successful authors who've already walked the path you want to travel. Now, pay attention to these few items:

- Cover design — How does it look? What's the tone? Is it the same as the others in the niche?

- Content — What's the writing style? Is it something you can do? Can you create something similar?

- Content length — How long is the content? How many pages?

- Reviews — What are readers saying about the book? What is missing from that book you can fulfill?

What a lot of authors fail to realize is marketing comes down to not just the content, but the outward appearance of that content and the way consumers perceive that content. Get it wrong, and no one will be interested. Get it right, and you're fast on your way to realizing success.

Once you nail down your marketing plan, what do you do to get your product seen? You promote it. This is the least sexy part of the business. Everyone loves to write a good book. Most everyone loves to get a stellar book cover for their publication, but few people like to promote their book. Why? Because it's not easy.

What stands in our way of selling more books and success is one simple concept – rejection. When only a few people buy your book, it seems like the world is rejecting your work. That sucks! No one likes rejection, much less the failure of never realizing success for all your hard work.

You're probably saying, "Dale, I don't have an issue with rejection."

Really? Then, what have you done to promote your book lately? How many sales did it garner? If it was a small number, how did you feel about it? It probably felt bad, almost the same feeling you get when someone rejects you. However, the good news is if you find a promotional strategy that works, no matter how small, then you've seen enough proof of concept to try it again. You'll just need to refine your approach or tweak your marketing to get better results.

To cement my argument about how authors don't like to market their book, I'll break down exactly what promotion is. When you promote your book, you're essentially sharing who you are, where you're at, and what you do. It leaves you in a vulnerable position. That's why it's never nice to have little to no results when promoting your book.

What we have to do is refine your approach to marketing and promotion. If you *only* get your brand on-point and your promotional plans dialed in, then you significantly increase your odds of success. Though you might feel strong in one area of marketing and promotion, I implore you to read all the way through and don't skip the content. I have a ton of information that'll start with the fundamentals and build up to more advanced tactics.

Without knowing what you should do to start, advanced strategies will never help you grow your author brand or sell more books. Quite a few authors get that wrong. You can't learn to fly until you learn the basics of how to crawl. First, let's undo some misunderstandings and exercise critical thinking about marketing and promoting books.

*A*fter six years of self-publishing and four years of teaching people how to do it, I've heard many of the same excuses for low book sales. I can usually track it back to bad marketing and promotion. Let me rephrase that for emphasis. Authors are not successful because they are not marketing and promoting their books properly.

When authors do a particular marketing and promotional strategy right, they drop the ball in another area – consistency. You must be consistent in your marketing and promotional efforts to see any real results. The business of self-publishing is a long game. Forget all the get-rich-quick dreams some random online hack has sold you. Dismiss any random interview you saw of an author who made $10,000 in their first 30 days. The vast majority of authors have to work their faces off to get anywhere in this business. And, they have to do it consistently over time to see any results.

Woody Allen once said, "Showing up is eighty percent of life." But, showing up just isn't enough to make an impact. You have to show up one hundred percent of the time consistently to see real results.

In fact, the old quote from Bruce Lee states it best when he said:

> I fear not the man who has practiced 10,000 kicks once, but I fear the man who has practiced one kick 10,000 times.

Bruce wasn't merely referring to martial arts. He focused more on what people do to achieve success. It goes beyond just doing one thing many times at one time. Success in business boils down to how much you put in consistently over time. So, if you want to achieve any modicum of success, you must commit to it, stick to it, never let up, and keep pushing forward.

All of this applies to marketing and promotion. It's not enough for you to put pen to paper and publish the content. If you expect anyone to find your work, you need to put in the most work after you've published your content. After all, publishing and praying alone will only get you so far. The whole process of marketing and promotion should begin well before you even put pen to paper.

When Should an Author Begin Marketing and Promotion?

What came first – the chicken or the egg? This analogy seems to play a huge part in determining when authors should begin marketing and promotion. Quite a few authors believe you can't be successful until you've published a book or a certain number of books. Then again, you can't get anyone to read your book unless you have a following either, right? Yes.

Even though you can leverage keywords to gain more discoverability on Amazon, you shouldn't rely solely on Amazon to do all the hard work for you. The fact is you are going to have to do 99.9% of the work, and it all starts right now. Whether you're a new author or a veteran self-publisher, it's up to you to build your following. But where do you start? How do you get a following if you don't have a book? Stay with me, because it's going to take some time to give you a full overhead view of what to do and where to go.

It's not as simple as saying:

> Do X, Y, and Z, and you'll be good to go.

There are far too many moving parts, so we'll have to chip away at this one swing at a time. In the meantime, know that marketing and promotion should start before you even put pen to paper. The hype train leaves the station as soon as you've internally committed to writing a book. That's all you need to know for right now.

Once you get started, publish your book, and you promote the launch, when do you stop? You stop once you've had enough. Famous brands like Nike and McDonald's never stop marketing and promoting. Why? They want the top spot as the foremost authority in their niche. These brands want to be the only viable option in athletic wear and fast food, respectively. You want the same for your book.

In fact, in an interview with a business strategies consultant, Jonny Andrews, I asked if one book was enough. He essentially said it is, but the promotional work is going to be far heavier than if the author had an entire backlog to send people to. That means if you decide to publish only one book, you'll need to put all your time, energy, and attention into building awareness around that book. The work never stops.

Should an Author Ever Stop?

In 2019, I faced the scary reality of what happens when I don't promote my books. I have a backlog of over forty different books in health and fitness, with thirty-eight titles translated into seven other languages. This brand of fitness books crushed it from 2016 to 2017, but it slowly died away. Why? Because my attention went elsewhere, and I stopped actively promoting these titles. Where these books had been pulling in substantial revenue, now they were hardly making any significant profits.

I discovered first-hand what comes from sitting back on my laurels and expecting the world to come to me. To my credit, I consciously walked away from the fitness brand in 2018 to focus on my career as a video content creator. I even admitted to myself I didn't care if the books died off. In reality, and subconsciously, I believed these books would continue to pull in the lion's share of the revenue.

When your product doesn't perform consistently or draw in enough sales on Amazon, the algorithm focuses on other products that will sell. Where my fitness books pulled in significant revenue at one point, other books since replaced them and made up for the loss in revenue. My books fell out of grace with the Amazon algorithm.

Momentum vs. Inertia with Marketing and Promotion

In 2016, my fitness brand was on fire. It seemed I could do no wrong with the Amazon algorithm. Heck, I didn't even have to touch Amazon Advertising at the time. I solely relied on external sources such as free book promotion websites, email marketing, and social media marketing to drive traffic to my books. Going into 2017, I stopped consistently promoting my books. I even gave up on using KDP Select for promoting my titles and decided to publish beyond the Amazon platform so I could gain more readers.

Though momentum worked in my favor from 2016 to 2017, the following year came with force equally powerful as momentum. It was inertia. That means my book sales slowed down and even came to a near halt. Trying to get momentum back in my favor would be a near-impossible task. Why? Because it's like I'm starting from scratch, except worse. The Amazon algorithm loves new products. It also loves proven products. To get back into the good graces of the Amazon algorithm, I'd need to prove myself all over again.

Much like pushing a giant snowball uphill, it'd be tough, but it wouldn't be impossible.

I gave each of my fitness books a facelift, changed the book descriptions, added a few new keywords, and then fired off new Amazon advertising campaigns. In truth, though, I'm merely using these books as a case study and a testing ground. As you can imagine, since you're reading a book about self-publishing, my direction is no longer with the fitness brand. Instead, I'm focused more on building the *Self-Publishing with Dale* brand. Rather than go back to something of mild interest, I'd rather pay the closest attention to what I can stick with for the long term. That means marketing and promoting consistently for the next few years and beyond.

I share my story to demonstrate the power of momentum versus inertia. The effectiveness of your marketing and promotional efforts relies heavily on whether you have momentum in your favor or if you're working against inertia. That's not to say you should quit if you have inertia working against you. It's merely to state you might have one heck of a hill to climb if you want to get anywhere with your promotional efforts. The best part is if you set up an author platform, it's much easier for you to keep the ball rolling and momentum working for you.

*A*fter the launch of Kindle Direct Publishing (KDP), the world's perception of self-publishing forever changed. No longer was self-publishing relegated to conversations surrounding your weird uncle who wrote, published, and bought a pallet-full of erotica books in his garage. Self-publishing became accessible to everyone. Authors who would otherwise get rejected by traditional publishing companies and agents could now skip the gatekeepers and publish their work themselves.

As the walls came crumbling down and ebooks stepped to the forefront of publishing, a new crop of entrepreneurs stepped up. Quite a few of them had the best intentions and are still running profitable self-publishing businesses. Simultaneously, another lot of get-rich-quick schemers and scammers saw the land of opportunity and loopholes to abuse in the system.

Since the Amazon algorithm could be used and abused, these bad actors found a way to publish content onto the Amazon platform quickly. They could easily fleece buyers of their money by putting out low-quality content with no real direction and the sole intent of making money. These efforts were at the expense of the customer.

As Amazon KDP matured, the algorithm and systems became more sophisticated. KDP closed loopholes abused by the bad actors. Naturally, as these bad actors saw they could no longer simply shotgun out dozens of books in a week based on various topics, they closed up shop and moved to the next big thing.

Meanwhile, authors who established themselves early on saw a big return on their early efforts. These authors wrote high-quality books, nurtured a growing readership, and focused on delivering value to their audience. These authors had momentum working in their favor and not merely loopholes that rewarded them.

What set these authors apart from the rest was how they stuck to it. They built a lasting presence and continued to do it despite all the changes through Amazon KDP. They created what is called an author platform, or I sometimes call it a brand.

An author platform is so much more than just a stage where an author speaks to his fans. It's a consistent message and placement of the message that makes up the author platform. The author platform can consist of:

- What readers expect

- Where they can find the author

- How they can rely on that author

- How they perceive the author

- When readers can expect to see the next release

The author platform can be as simple as:

- An author website

- A marketplace to buy their books

- Social media presence

- Any miscellaneous ways readers can find the author

- Places where the readers can interact with the author—online forums, social media, etc.

The authors who confidently march forward into battle and never let up are rewarded in the long term, so long as they stay true to their author platform and brand. If they don't deviate from their mission, stay true to their audience, and consistently promote their platform, they'll win big. We're in the age of the brand and author platform. Amazon loves to reward authors who put in the work and bring in the audience. Nothing attracts a crowd like a crowd. The only way to draw in that crowd is to build an author platform.

Where do you start building an author platform? How do you build a brand that lasts? What are the first best steps to establishing your author presence?

Building a brand seems simple in theory, but in practice, it's much harder to fire off. Before you can ever consider making any significant impact on your author earnings, you need to consider the impact you'll make in the world.

In *Amazon Keywords for Books*, I shared how my first book was my worst book. To say it was hammered garbage is mildly offending to dumpster fires throughout the world. I believed I wrote a book for everyone. Once a friend opened my eyes to the error of my ways, I found I'd written a book for no one. Because when you try to please everyone, you please no one in the process.

Before you write your next book, I want you to consider a few things:

1. Who is your audience?

2. What is your message?

3. How is your message relevant to your intended audience?

4. Can your audience rely on you to be steadfast in what you provide?

Imagine visiting your local shoe store to pick up some new footwear. Your expectation when you arrive is you'll browse the selection of shoes, find what you're looking for, try on a few pairs, and then hope-fully buy something. What if you showed up to your local shoe store only to discover they're now selling pizza? No, they don't sell shoes, even though their name would imply otherwise. No, they won't make a special order for you, because they're no longer selling shoes. If you want pizza, they're your place. If you want shoes, well, you're out of luck.

When you go to a shoe store, you expect to buy shoes. That's how a brand works. A brand is an unwritten promise with the world of what you deliver and what they can expect. If you can't get good on that promise and stay consistent with what they've come to expect, you're in real trouble.

Your brand is essentially your promise. It boils down to:

- Your appearance

- Your message

- Your core values

- Your deliverables

Brand-building is now more critical than ever because we're in the age of technology. Search engine algorithms dominate our lives online. If you want your audience to hear you above the online noise, then you need to build a brand. Your brand's message needs to be consistent across the board.

Much like I shared how Amazon rewards consistent performing products, most search engines do the same. If you're the expert and go-to authority in underwater basket weaving for dolphins, then stick to it. After you've been at it for a few years and have consistently promoted your brand, then you'll earn the favor of most any search engine.

Where do you start? What are the things you need in place? Well, you need to know who you are. For simplicity's sake, let's focus on you as an author. Your author name should be prime real estate when it comes to building a brand. Whether you're using a pen name or your given name, this is probably the best step forward.

The first step you need to take is to own all properties containing your name. That means you need to take your virtual flag and place it in the sand on a website domain name and throughout social media. Even if you don't plan to use social media, you still need to take it. You're planning for the next five years. If you're working with my plan, then that includes going big or going home. We go big every time. Take the social media handles; that way, it safeguards you later when bad actors try to impersonate you.

Bad news if you're name is Michael Johnson (sorry, Uncle Mike, but it's true) – it's going to be tough finding just the right domain name and social media presence. If you're an author, then chances are you have creativity on your side.

Choosing a Domain Name & Social Media Handles

I can hear the collective groan from some of you. Yep, getting a website is mission-critical for establishing your brand. Part of having and running a professional website includes having an author-specific domain name. No, you're not going to rely on free hosting with Wix and their unmemorable long URL. I take no issue with free site hosting, but you need to make it easy for any reader to discover you or find you after reading your book. They can't find you if your web address is MichaelHJohnsonHotAuthor.Wix.com. At that point, you're promoting Wix's brand, not your author brand. No offense to Wix, but I'm not in the business to promote Wix when building my author brand.

The next thing to consider is social media names, also known as handles. If you skip this part, I promise you will regret it later. Eventually, as your author brand picks up steam, you're going to have some random person take your name. And, in some instances, they might even assume your identity and impersonate you. It sucks! So, safeguard your brand, and your future self will thank you.

What social media platforms will you need? It depends a lot on where your audience is. Rather than getting hung up on the details, I'd recommend you reserve as many of them as possible. Just be sure to use all the same login names and store all your passwords safely.

Visit NameCheck.com to find out the availability of your brand name. I've used this site quite a few times to help coaching students reserve their names. It's free to use and will quickly show you where your name is available. You simply type in your name and press Enter to see what is or is not available.

My primary concern is if the domain name is available. I'd recommend keeping your domain name simple. Do not complicate it with acronyms, numbers, or symbols. You need a domain name that's is easy to say and remember. For example, my author name is Dale L. Roberts. Naturally, readers will recognize my name from my book as Dale L. Roberts. My domain name of DaleLRoberts.com is simple and easy to remember. That's what you want to do.

A coaching student once reserved a complex domain name having little to do with her author name. Heck, it wasn't even a word, but more of an acronym for something that seemed like an inside joke. It went something like ADFXBooksToWeightLoss.com. Insert my perplexed look here. Confused by the name, I asked her what it meant. She explained the meaning behind the name and was confident readers would remember it. Nearly three years later, this author hasn't gone anywhere with her brand. Why? She hedged all her bets on a name no one would remember, much less know.

If you're shooting for using your author name and it's taken, then try different variations of your first, middle, and last name. Try to add "the" or "author" as a prefix in the domain name. It's going to take time. Once you've found a good domain name, reach out to any number of domain name registrars online. You can usually find a domain for about $17 per year. Choose your service provider wisely and check their reviews before investing your money in them.

Now comes the social media aspect of things. It's okay if you can't get your domain name to precisely match your social media handles. Just remember, any time you have deviation, you have to build more awareness. That's why if you choose a social media handle, keep it consistent across the board. Again, I know you love your name and want to use it, but if someone already has Brenda Smith , then you need to come up with something creative while still honoring your brand.

I'd recommend, at the very least, having your social media handles match on Twitter, Facebook, Instagram, LinkedIn, and YouTube. These are currently the major social media platforms. If you see a smaller, less-known social media platform on the list for NameCheck.com, then use your best judgment on whether you should or shouldn't open an account there.

Once you've unearthed a good fit, it's time to open and reserve the social media accounts. It will take a little time. Go to each platform and at least provide the necessary information and your author picture. If you don't have a professional headshot, then have someone shoot one for you and upload that as a placeholder. Once you get a professional headshot, you can go back through the platforms and upload it.

The most important part of setting up these social media profiles is brand congruency. Make sure your name is the same, the look is the same, and your message is the same. Make your message very clear where you have the opportunity. In some instances, like Twitter, you can do that in your description. It could be something as simple as:

Keep your Twitter profile clean and the images brand relevant.

You'll notice, I'm brief and don't go overboard. If you spend hours crafting long-form copy, the chances are likely your potential reader will not take the time to read it. Be precise about who you are, what you do, and what people can expect. Think of your description as an introduction to someone you just met. You don't want to make your first impression one where you're bloviating for hours at a time while your new-found acquaintance tunes you out. It's a simple conversation.

"What do you do, Dale?" asks my visitor.

"I'm an indie author, video content creator, and self-publishing advocate. What do you do?" I reply.

The most important step is to secure these social media profiles, not make them perfect. In due time, you'll change your profile image and refine your descriptions and bios. For now, just secure them, put in placeholders, and get ready for the next steps.

Just remember to keep brand congruency. When someone sees you on Instagram, they need to see the same thing on Twitter, Facebook, LinkedIn, YouTube, and beyond. That way, it's a familiar face, and there's no doubt that it's you who runs the profile.

Once you have your domain name and social media presence, you've done the basics. The whole point is you want to be easily accessible and discoverable online. This plays an important part not only in discovery but as an insurance policy. In the event Amazon kicks you off their platform, your readers will know where to find you. With a website and social media, your audience won't ever lose track of you.

Speaking of Amazon, let's get a look under the hood and find out how to best leverage the online juggernaut to build and grow your author platform. It's not going to be easy, but with a few simple steps and best practices, you'll be on your way to building an unstoppable author brand.

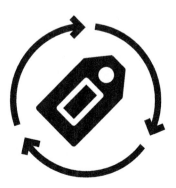

*E*veryone admires or loves a winner. There are few exceptions to this rule. When it comes to gaining the favor of a search engine algorithm, it's no different. Search engines function on a highly complex mathematical formula called an algorithm. How search queries get results is based in large part on:

- The overall customer experiences

- Previous browsing history

- Previous consuming behaviors

- Similar audience behaviors

Amazon's search engine algorithm is a fickle beast. Just when you think you gained its favor, it dumps you like a bad habit. One way you can coax the beast and win its love is through cold, hard, and consistent sales. How do you sell more books then? What do you need to do to sell books consistently?

At first, selling books is easy. After all, most everyone has a friend or family member willing to support the cause. However, once you burn through your inner circle contacts list, where do you go? Oddly enough, there's a much bigger world out there beyond your inner circle. All you have to do is be willing to step outside your comfort zone to welcome them in.

The bottom line, when it comes to gaining the favor of the Amazon algorithm, is to sell books. Because once you sell more books, Amazon will push your books to more customers who'll hopefully buy your books. Then, it becomes one beautifully rewarding cycle.

Amazon will push your book through a variety of avenues, including on their website through these options:

- Customers Also Bought

- Books You Might Like

- Frequently Bought Together

They'll also serve your book to their email subscribers and Kindle readers. There's no real way of guaranteeing Amazon will do this for you, and there's no set metric of how many sales you have to get before they start serving your book to other readers.

How Amazon Will NOT Build Your Audience for You

Amazon is in the business of selling products, not in the business of building other people's businesses. To be frank, Amazon is not your friend. They're merely a platform that fulfills customer orders. The online retailer is there for the customer and not you. It's a symbiotic relationship, though. If you were running a successful author brand through your site and Amazon chose to distribute or advertise through you, who would you honor more - your following or Amazon?

The answer is simple – your audience. Because your following is responsible for where you are and what you can do as an author, don't take it personally when Amazon doesn't prioritize your amazing epic novel about honey badgers and warlocks.

If Amazon sees some promise in your product, then they'll push it to the customers they see most fit for consuming it. If that audience doesn't buy, then you'll be at odds with the almighty algorithm. It's a sad reality. Amazon wants you to make sales. You must prove your worth before it even begins to get behind you.

Amazon will not build your audience for you. It's on you to do that. In the early days of Kindle Publishing, you could get away with finding a profitable keyword with low competition. Then, people would discover you easily, and you could run roughshod on the whole niche. Not anymore.

The Amazon Algorithm grows more sophisticated by the day, and the end goal of that algorithm is – customer satisfaction. Customers can't be satisfied if they search for a solution to their problems and go away empty-handed. That is a huge reason why I suggest authors to not rely on Amazon to push their book. You need to be the biggest cheerleader for your book because Amazon won't be until you've proven yourself.

That's why publishing and praying is not a reliable promotional strategy. Relying on outside forces to handle your marketing is a recipe for disaster. The few people who do succeed with this strategy are the unicorns of this business. Over 99% of authors need a solid approach to marketing, and it all starts with what you do off Amazon and before you launch your book.

All About Relevancy, Baby

In my book *Amazon Keywords for Books*, I discuss relevancy and how it works with search engines. The best way to establish relevance is through sales. Other factors play a role in building relevance for your title. After all, the more relevant your title is on Amazon, the more it'll serve your book to customers.

What if you're having no sales or minimal sales? How do you build relevance on your title? Beyond what I'm going to share in marketing and promotional strategies, you need to bear in mind one thing. Amazon loves new products, and it also loves products with refreshed data. If your book isn't faring so hot after thirty to ninety days, consider giving it a facelift.

A few ways you can breathe a little life back into your books is through the book cover. If you find your sales slumping, sometimes a new cover might be the trick to grab the attention of browsing customers. You might believe your book isn't appearing to customers. Believe it or not, Amazon does its part to place your product in front of potential buyers based on a few factors:

1. The customer's buying history

2. The customer's search history

3. Customers with similar buy & search history

4. Your book's keywords and category selection

With millions of customers visiting at any given moment on Amazon, I'm hard-pressed in thinking your book hasn't appeared in front of someone in some capacity. This is why an eye-catching, genre-specific cover is imperative to getting your ideal reader's attention. Get it wrong, and they'll scroll right past your book and never give it a second look. Get it right, and they'll at least visit your product page.

The next part is where your book could be failing to build relevancy – the book description. If you cannot give the browsing customer a compelling reason to buy your book, they'll most likely move onto other things. Sure, the Amazon algorithm likes when someone clicks on your book's product page link when brought up in a search query. Even better, the algorithm loves when a click leads to a sale.

How do you go from getting no sales to some sales? Improve your book's metadata, including:

1. Title, subtitle, series name

2. Book description

3. Seven backend keywords

4. Category placement

Update your metadata and allow Amazon to showcase your work to a different subset of customers. Once given the opportunity, you should hopefully see better results. If not, then you need to lean on more external factors. This means you don't go back and change your metadata again. Constantly changing your metadata confuses the algorithm and tosses your work into a mess of other confusing books.

The Publishing & Republishing Method

As mentioned previously, Amazon loves new products. It likes to test new products with its buyers to see if it'll take off and provide a larger bottom line. That's a huge reason why Amazon has a special subcategory for the bestseller's lists called Hot New Releases. This list consists of the bestselling print books and ebooks published in the last thirty days for a given category.

Amazon uses the Hot New Releases category to showcase the best performing books published in the last 30 days.

The Hot New Release bestseller list showcases what's performing best right now. It allows them to shine since already established books dominate the top of the bestseller's list for most categories. Otherwise, your book can't be heard above the noise and hit the top of the bestseller's lists. In a way, the Hot New Release lists level the playing field and provides an opportunity for newbies to shine. Think of it like open mic night, and you're finally getting your chance to sing for a willing audience.

What happens after the first thirty days is where it gets tricky. If you didn't prove your worth or take advantage of the spotlight, the Amazon algorithm is quick to discard your book and focus on the next shiny object and new release. You might notice the first thirty days to be beautiful while getting consistent sales beyond your wildest dreams. Then, day thirty-one comes, and your sales drop a little, followed by day thirty-two when you see even less. Day after day, week after week, your book drops in sales and sinks into obscurity.

At this point, you'll want to look into updating your book metadata. With ebooks, it's relatively simple to edit the title, subtitle, series name, and more. It's a bit more problematic when you want to update the same info on your print book since that information is static based on the ISBN (International Book Standard Number). That's okay because, in most instances, a slight adjustment in your book description and keyword choice could make all the difference.

I wouldn't recommend delisting your work and then republishing it. The problem is you erase all relevancy for that title and are starting over from scratch. Yes, inertia is a pain, but at least you have a proven commodity with some sales history. Once you delist that book and publish it anew, you're starting over and never really know what worked and what didn't.

Adjust the book metadata and wait. You must understand the effectiveness does not show in real-time. You can't change a book description and expect it to prove effective within twenty-four hours. Give your book time and breathing room. Allow the changes to take place at least thirty to ninety days before considering another change. It gives the algorithm time to know your product and test it in front of potential buyers.

Yes, the thirty-day window of a new release is nice! It's not the solution to a book that's not selling. The solution to a book not selling is creating a better book cover, crafting a better book description, and promoting the heck out of that book.

The Delisting & Republishing Scam to Avoid

About three or four years ago, a popular YouTube personality and go-to expert in self-publishing taught her coaching students to rely heavily on the thirty-day window. If a book did well beyond the thirty-day window, then she'd have her students leave it alone. However, if sales dip at all beyond the first thirty days, she'd have them delist the title and republish it. The book was the same title with no deviation or change. In fact, it wasn't even a second edition.

The problem was two-fold:

1. Authors were gaming the system to get exposure instead of doing real marketing and promotion.

2. Customers thought the book was new despite it being a rerun.

This doesn't even address how some of these books had terrible reviews. Once the author delists the books, the bad reviews disappear, and the title reappears without a scratch. This is a bad business practice. If your title has low reviews, then you're doing something wrong. Merely delisting the title to remove bad reviews covers up your inadequacy to provide quality content readers want. Don't do this. If your book has low reviews, then the best thing to do is either delist the title and rewrite the entire thing or improve it and upload the updated version.

The latter option doesn't seem like fun, but you keep the history and relevance of the title. You also aren't duping the customers into buying your book despite having low reviews. Address the bad reviews by providing a better reading experience.

Thankfully, about two years ago, this self-publishing coach stopped teaching her students to game the system. She had them embrace better business practices like writing better content, executing sound promotional strategies, and building an author brand. Kudos to her!

Amazon Author Central — The Onsite Author Profile

Hey, even if you skipped my advice for getting a website and domain name, you've always got Amazon Author Central. While I lead you to believe Amazon isn't your friend, they are still committed to equipping you with the right tools to become successful. It's just up to you to use those tools to the best of their abilities. One of those tools is Amazon Author Central.

When you publish your book to the Amazon platform, the website indexes your content, including all the metadata. Indexing is the process of storing your product data, so it's discoverable through their search engine.

What if you could index your product beyond just the one time? Imagine being able to have your book more discoverable by listing it twice. That's not out of the realm of possibilities since Amazon Author Central is your solution.

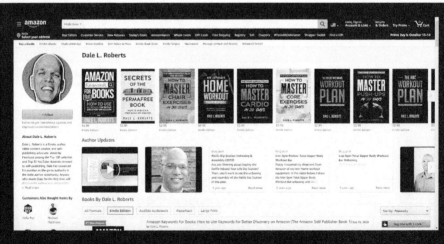

An Amazon author profile is an excellent way for readers to see all your books in one spot.

Amazon Author Central is a way for authors to set up a profile related to their writing. The profile showcases your information on a customizable webpage with:

- An author bio

- An author picture

- All of the author's books

- Blog posts — You can link your blog but only do it if it's relevant to your niche. There's no sense in adding to the noise and cluttering up your page.

- Videos and pictures — do you have any promotional videos or graphics? Here's the spot to showcase it. If you made a book trailer, then your author profile is the spot to share it.

- A follow feature — visitors can follow a profile for notifications on new releases

Author Central also provides a suite of tools that help you optimize your book listing you can't otherwise do in your KDP dashboard. Think about all the missed opportunities you have when you only have seven backend keywords limited to fifty characters. That's okay! Now you can use Author Central for those missed keywords and discoverability.

This free option available to all authors with books published on Amazon (regardless of distribution management) has:

- Historical book sales rank tracking

- Additional metadata for all books including:

  - Editorial reviews

> Dustjacket metadata

> Miscellaneous information

- Regional sales tracking — this feature is nice if you want to know where you get a lot of sales to remarket & retarget buyers in a given region.

- And, more

Amazon Author Central is more than just a
place to set up your author profile.

Think of Author Central as a social media feature for Amazon. It allows readers another opportunity to see all your work showcased in one spot. It also allows you more customizable features on your product page, allowing you more opportunities for discovery.

Much like when you set up your social media profiles, you'll want to do the same with your author profile. Upload the same headshot you did for your social media profiles. Remember, brand congruency is mission-critical. People need to be able to spot your brand at a glance much in the same way someone sees the golden arches, and they think McDonald's. When someone sees the swoosh, they think Nike. Your headshot should be instant recognition. Engrain your pretty mug into people's minds to remember who you are as an author and brand.

Next, you'll want to create a short bio relevant to your niche. Far too often, I see struggling authors using this space to showcase their entire life. Don't do that. Only share information that is relevant to your niche. If you have a degree in exercise science and you're a fitness author, then certainly add that to your bio. However, if you're a science fiction fantasy writer, don't share it. Having a degree in exercise science has little to do with sci-fi fantasy.

When crafting your bio, don't worry about whether to write in first person or third person. The point is to write the best ad copy you can that paints an accurate picture of you. That way, random visitors and readers have a better insight into you as an author. Like a good book description, lead with a good opening hook. Then, craft short, punchy sentences readers can relate to. Keep your bio short to about 200-300 words. Anything longer is just extraneous.

Lastly, claim all your publications to post them on your profile. Once you claim your books, they'll all display neatly at the top of your page with the most popular publication on the left and the least popular on the right. Again, Amazon helps you out and showcasing what is most popular, so more buyers want to purchase your book.

Once you have everything set, Amazon will allow you to set a customized URL based on your author name. Choose what best fits, but don't get too hung up on it. Once you get a customized URL from Amazon, you can simply add a domain name, subdomain, or subdirectory to redirect to your Amazon profile.

For instance, to get to my author profile, I tell readers to visit DaleLRoberts.com/Amazon. This subdirectory redirects to the custom URL Author Central gave me of amazon.com/author/daleroberts. The custom URL is all well and good, but it's a bit harder to communicate and commit to memory than the URL redirect.

If you need further help with setting up your Amazon Author Central Profile, visit my video series at DaleLinks.com/AuthorCentral.

Remember how I had you reserve a domain name? Now it's time to put it to work. You need a safe space for your author brand. Think of it as your safe house in case anything goes sideways on any distribution platform. As a best practice, having a website gives you one spot to send all readers and visitors. Your website acts as a hub for all things involving your brand.

Did you have an interview recently? Great, showcase it on your website. Do you have a new release and want to announce it? Awesome! Showcase it on your website. Are you launching a podcast for your niche and unsure how to let people know? Excellent! Send people to your website.

Your website is the single most effective tool for your entire brand. If there's one area you should invest in, make it your website. It's where readers, brands, companies, and services can find you. As a bonus, it's an easy way to get people to remember your brand.

By now, you should have a general grasp of why you should get a domain name that's author specific. Let's discuss why you should invest just a little more and get site hosting. Can you get away with hosting your website through free services like Blogger, WordPress, or Wix? Sure! While you skirt the additional cost of hosting, you're greatly hindering your ability to be discovered through search engines.

Besides, nothing screams amateur hour like a website with another company's brand stamped all over it. Those services are free for a good reason – they get to promote your product and data mine your visitors. Yep, it's not a conspiracy theory. If you're driving traffic to your free website, you're doing it at the expense of your visiting audience. The service can remarket and retarget your audience without you having any say. The sad part is you're complicit because you didn't invest in premium site hosting.

I understand if you're cash-strapped and need a cost-effective solution. I highly recommend building in costs when launching your author brand for a domain name and site hosting. Between the two products, you can spend about $130 per year. That runs about $10.83 per month. If you sold about two books at a profit of $6, then you've already paid for it every month. You can sell two books per month, right? If not, continue reading, and you'll find out how.

When it comes to the right company to buy a domain name and site hosting, do your research. Ask around and see what most authors prefer. I don't want to lead you in one direction or the other. At the moment, I'm looking to move away from my current hosting service due to some complications (see here: DaleLinks.com/Hacked). I'll be the first to tell you websites are not my forte, and I wouldn't even know a TPS Report from a PHP. If you do enough research, you'll find a few features in common and the cost of the services.

Most website hosting packages run anywhere from $60 to $120 per year. Based on how much content you plan to put on your site, you may need to get a more expensive hosting package. Let's say you're an author with a background in photography. Chances are likely that you're going to need a bit more for your site to manage larger picture files.

Conversely, some fiction authors won't need much. If you're only show-casing front cover images and author signings, then you only need a basic site hosting package, nothing too elaborate. Either way, if you're unfamiliar, I'd recommend starting at the most basic website hosting package, and you can always upgrade when you need it.

Plan an expense every year for your website hosting and domain name. Many authors forget about these expenses. When it comes time to pay the bill, they become delinquent or shut down their site. That's a horrible situation, especially if you pick up enough authority and search engines index your content. You leave your domain name open to bad actors who'll buy up your property. Then, when you need it, they'll sell it to you at a higher premium. Don't let it escalate to that point.

Having a website isn't essential, but it is necessary to build a lasting presence online without the aid of social media and retail platforms. Ultimately, your website is your safe space. If social media shuts you down or puts you off, you can always send your readers and followers to your website. If an online retail platform decides for whatever reason they've had enough of your books and kicks you off, then readers will know precisely where to find you.

Too many authors romanticize the business of self-publishing through platforms like Amazon or its competitors. They believe this train will go on forever. And, for most, it will. For a select few, Amazon has the sole discretion to kick them off. They do not need a reason to do so. It's their sandbox, and we're merely playing in it.

Last year, a friend mentioned how a mutual acquaintance fell on hard times. In the previous years, this author was building a six-figure per month romance publishing business. He had all his eggs in the Amazon basket. Though he allegedly was doing everything by the book, Amazon terminated his account. He didn't have a website. He didn't even have a mailing list. This author had nothing and nowhere for his readers to know where to begin to find him.

Imagine making over $100,000 per month in revenue and not pulling out an insurance policy as a safeguard for worst-case scenarios. If this author had only put together an email list, he could send subscribers to his website. With six-figures in revenue, he had the readers. He could rely entirely on his website to fulfill orders. Yet he naively relied on Amazon to be there for him forever.

Don't rely on Amazon for everything, folks. The reality is Amazon isn't your friend. They're merely a platform you can leverage to build your author platform. Conversely, you are also a tool they use to get more sales. When you understand publishing on Amazon is merely a transactional relationship, you'll take better steps to safeguard your business. One of those first steps is to set up your author website today!

Amazon Associates - Getting Paid for Selling Your Books

You might be a little confused seeing a section about getting paid for selling your books in a chapter about marketing through your website. Stick with me on this one, because it requires a deeper explanation. You're already getting paid to sell your books, so what's the big deal with Amazon Associates?

A few years ago, I'd stumbled on some fine print on Amazon Author Central. In the Author Central dashboard, you'll see recommendations for making the most of your product listing on Amazon. In one single line, you might notice Author Central recommends something called Amazon Associates.

Amazon Associates is an affiliate marketing platform where Amazon pays you to advertise their products. What is affiliate marketing, you might ask? Affiliate marketing is where a company or service will pay you for referring people to them. Sometimes you will be paid for simply referring new customers, and most of the time, you will be paid for referring paid customers.

Here's how affiliate marketing works. I watched and enjoyed the latest movie with Dwayne "The Rock" Johnson. When I finished watching it, I told my friends they should go check it out. Under normal circumstances, I get nothing out of the referral. I only get the satisfaction of sharing a good movie-going experience with a friend.

Imagine getting paid for sending your friends to watch The Rock's latest movie. What if you got paid for sending people to that theater even if they didn't end up watching The Rock's movie? Affiliate marketing works in the same way.

If you like a service, product, or company, you can align yourself with that company through an affiliate program. Any time you send traffic or paying customers, you get a small percentage of the sale. The best part is the referred customers don't pay any more for the services than they normally would while you get a small kickback. Pretty neat, right?

The Amazon Associates program works in the same way; however, what the customer buys will dictate how much you get paid.

"Wait, Dale. Didn't you say I'd get paid more for selling my books?"

I'm glad you asked because you get paid in two of three ways.

1. You get paid a royalty for the sale of the book through KDP.

2. You get paid a percentage of the sale price on Amazon (typically 4%).

3. You get paid for any other sales made on the platform 24 hours after the customer uses your referral link.

The last part is one that blows everyone's minds. First, referring traffic to your book is a given. If you aren't sending traffic and potential readers to your book on Amazon, then we need to fix that right now. Next, you get paid a percentage of the sale price. That percentage is like Amazon giving you a cut of their take just for being a good sport and sending customers. Last, even if a customer doesn't buy your book, but they buy a product on Amazon, you get compensation.

Wild, right? Let's say you send people to buy your book. The customer doesn't buy your book but gets other items. When they make that purchase, you get a small commission. In a best-case scenario, the referred customer buys your book and products, thereby increasing your affiliate earnings.

How do you get an Amazon Associates account? It's not easy, but it's simple. You'll need…wait for it…a website! Ding ding ding! Hence why I inserted this subchapter about Amazon Associates in the chapter about building a website.

Visit affiliate-program.amazon.com to apply for an account. It's a rather lengthy process but somewhat intuitive. Though you get instant access to creating affiliate links, you should hold off. Wait to set up an Amazon Associates account until you have one thing dialed in – your website.

Amazon wants you to be their little worker bee and drive as many microtransactions as possible. The more worker bees they have out there, the more money you both earn. Amazon is a publicly-traded company and doesn't just want anyone sending traffic. They have specific standards they like to adhere to. Rather than go through their entire terms of services, guidelines, and policies, I'll give you the important, need to know facts.

One of the main requirements Amazon has is affiliates need to have a website or online presence to drive traffic. They want proof of concept. Having any old micro-website won't do. Amazon wants you to advertise their product, but not have that be the only thing you do. After all, they're doing a damned good job at advertising their website. Why do they need another website that does the same? You're not different.

That's why it's paramount you build out your website with content. Fill your website with relevant content about you. Here are a few suggestions to include in your website to increase your chances of entering and staying in the Amazon Associates program:

1. **Welcome Page** — This is simply your website's main landing page. You should have your author name, a picture of you, and/or your latest book. Then let them know what they can expect on your website.

2. **About Page** — Showcase who you are through a professional headshot and well-written author bio. You may want to include contact information or relevant social media links.

3. **Contact Page** — Set up a simple contact form, so you don't have your email out there for spammers and hackers to get. Most web forms are free and integrate well with website hosting services.

4. **Blog** — You're an author, so act like one! I'm not telling you to write blog posts every day in perpetuity. Simply create about six to twelve different posts trickled out over about two to four

weeks. First, the blog posts aid in discoverability on Google and other search engines. Next, you showcase your writing skills and can promote your backlog of books. Lastly, you have content for people to consume that isn't just a bunch of affiliate links.

5. **Bookshelf** — This is simply a recommendation and not a necessity. This webpage showcases all your publications with Amazon product page links. Since you went through the trouble of creating an author website and writing a book, you might as well showcase your work. The best part is you can later use your bookshelf to insert your Amazon Associates links.

Need to Know Info about Amazon Associates

Once you get a website set up like previously mentioned and you've applied for your account, wait for approval from Amazon Associates. They'll typically email you within one to two weeks after applying. If you don't hear back right away, be patient.

A while ago, I was working on a side project with a close friend. With a customized domain name on a simple website, we set up an Amazon Associates account. Rather than wait for the approval, we created links through Amazon and posted them to our website. We were getting sales, and our Amazon Associates dashboard showed a nice return.

Within a week or two, we received the bad news. Amazon rejected our application based on the lack of available content on our website. We essentially didn't have enough meat on the bones for our website. Again, Amazon doesn't want your site to be solely their website links. They want you to be an actual legit website devoted to other things beyond selling Amazon's wares.

Equipped with this information, my friend and I got quickly to work and created about twelve blog posts we fired off daily for two weeks. It was enough content to prove we were more than an Amazon link dumping ground. We reapplied, waited two weeks, and Amazon sent an approval email.

What You Should & Shouldn't Do

The most critical step many affiliate marketers make is in fully disclosing the nature of the links. You can't simply rely on people to know what affiliate links are. You need to tell people in a public space on your website the nature of your relationship with Amazon, what the links lead to, and how it compensates you for sharing it. Sadly, this isn't so much an Amazon rule, but more a Federal Trades Commission (FTC) rule.

Since you're sending visitors to another site where you get paid for them visiting or buying something, you must tell your visitors that. You can simply do it in the post showcasing the link, or create a separate page with the disclosure. If you're doing the latter option, use a link to direct visitors for the full disclosure. Doing both will not hurt, and I even recommend it, so you aren't caught off guard.

Some people believe since you're getting paid for referring traffic that it influences your decision to promote a given product or service. In this case, it affects your decision. You're sending traffic to buy your book. You're getting paid more for it! Why wouldn't you be inclined to send people?! Just simply state something like:

> Full disclosure: The outbound link is part of an affiliate program where I'm compensated for any sales. This does not change the pricing for customers and greatly helps support this website.

Don't go overboard, and don't sweat it if anyone tries to call you on being a shill for Amazon. If you're going to have your book on Amazon, you might as well get paid for it. And, if you're going to promote your book on Amazon, you might as well get paid even more for it. After all, most customers aren't simply going to stop after buying your book. You sent a warm buyer into Amazon's hands. So, you might as well reap the rewards for sending the traffic and all the previous work of writing and publishing your book.

Creating a link can be somewhat confusing at first. You don't just want to sign up for Amazon Associates and then copy the URL in the browser. That's something you can do without Amazon Associates. With the program, you'll want to enable SiteStripe for Amazon Associates. Once enabled, visit Amazon.com and search for your book. Find your book, go to its product page. Then, click **Text** below **Get link** in the top left corner of SiteStripe. A pop-up window will show a highlighted short link—press **CTRL** and the letter **C** to copy it.

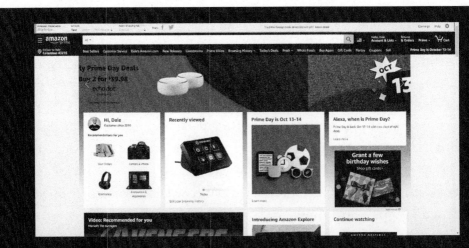

SiteStripe is the gray strip at the top of the Amazon browser when you're signed in as an Amazon Associate.

Then, go to where you wish to share the link—press **CTRL** and the letter **V** to paste it where you want. Now, when someone clicks that link, they'll be sent to Amazon and will be earmarked as your referred customer. This marking doesn't last forever and has a limited reach (about twenty-four hours). But, during that time, if a customer comes back and orders a product through Amazon, you get credit for it. That's regardless of it being your book or not.

Now, don't make the same mistake I did for my first few years of using Amazon Associates. According to their guidelines, you must use the exact link given to you. You cannot create a subdirectory, subdomain, or link shorteners (i.e., bitly, etc.) to redirect customers to Amazon. Though you might think how you send traffic isn't a big deal, some bad actors find nefarious ways to game the system. Rather than getting lumped in with that lot, stick to the rules.

That's probably one of the main reasons why Amazon doesn't want their links covered. Ever since learning I could not create domain redirects, I've done my best to correct course and strictly use Amazon's short links. The nice part about using Amazon short links is most people can tell it's an Amazon link. That's instant credibility and assurance the customer isn't visiting a sketchy website.

SiteStripe also has two social media buttons integrated into the dash. If you want to share your link via Facebook or Twitter, all you have to do is click the button, and you'll be whisked away to the respective platform. Then, customize your message and post it.

The biggest takeaway when it comes to using Amazon Associates is to be obvious. Share the link as it is and disclose the nature of the link. Don't go overboard with your links and beat people up 24/7 with it. Use it tastefully, and you'll see big returns with consistent efforts over the long haul.

49

Additional features in the Amazon Associates program make the program all the more rewarding but be selective. For instance, bounty programs give you more money for referrals. Amazon sets up special bonus rewards every few months for specific product types. If you're new to Amazon Associates, I'd recommend keeping it simple. Don't spread yourself too thin with all the features.

Ad embedding is one advertising feature Amazon offers. Having the ability to embed Amazon ads is nice, but you have to ask yourself, "What would my visitor think?" Is your website visitor supposed to focus on you or focus on buying products on another site?

Embedding Amazon widgets is nice, but I don't recommend it for a few reasons:

1. It distracts from your brand and sends visitors off your website. Most widgets display products that are not your books. Do you want to sell more books or sell other people's products?

2. The embedded widgets can slow down your website load time. Some visitors don't like waiting an extra three seconds while your Amazon widget populates on the page.

3. Having ads all over your website can make your website appear cluttered like a disorganized yard sale.

For me, I do not like putting the Amazon widget on my website. I did it for a hot minute on my fitness website, but then I started thinking about the visitor's first impression. Do I want first-time visitors to remember Amazon or me? I'll take the latter over the former. No one needs help remembering Amazon. Take every advantage you can get when it comes to your website.

Remember, with your website, less is more. This isn't just regarding Amazon widgets; it also includes your books and product recommendations. If you're going to use the Amazon Associates links, choose one page for all your relevant links. This is where a virtual bookshelf comes in handy. If you must include affiliate links on any pages of your bookshelf, limit how many you use to about one to two. Using too many affiliate links across your entire site can work against you.

This isn't so much to make a cleaner visiting experience. It's also due in large part to significant changes in the Google search engine algorithm. Google wants to send you traffic, but it will only trust websites it knows visitors will enjoy and consume. The name of the game on Google is data mining. If Google sends a customer to your website and the customer leaves, Google is less apt to send more customers. With a shorter customer experience on your website, Google has less data about that customer who used their search engine.

Conversely, when a customer visits your website and stays on your website longer, then Google deems your site to have more relevance based on your given topic. Having many affiliate links can be off-putting to visitors and create a disjointed customer journey that's hard for Google to track. Many industry experts state having too many affiliate links all over your site can be detrimental to long-term website discoverability and relevance.

The lesson is don't go buck wild on your affiliate links. You don't want your author platform to take a backseat to your affiliate marketing efforts. Select your affiliate links wisely, post them on one page, and if you must share any links outside your main affiliate link page, keep it to one to two links.

Lastly, avoid sharing Amazon Associates links in your email marketing efforts. Some email marketing platforms forbid any affiliate links in email broadcasts. Be careful about what you share in your email campaigns. We'll briefly touch on email marketing later in the book. Just remember the primary purpose of email marketing is to build a relationship with your subscriber. You can't build a good long-term relationship if all you do is assault the subscriber with nothing but affiliate links.

Simply leverage email marketing as a way to deliver traffic to your website. From there, let your website do all the heavy lifting. On your site, you can share your Amazon associates link or any other affiliate link. Besides, you give your email subscriber the option to view your offer or not. Giving your customer the higher ground builds more trust in the long run.

*L*et's get one thing straight. When it comes to social media marketing and promotion, I'm not the foremost expert. I know enough to make me dangerous. To be honest, no single methodology will be right or wrong. Telling you exactly how you should conduct yourself on social media is like trying to mold you into another version of me. You need to find your way and discover your voice.

One thing is for certain, social media is here to stay and has become an integral part of most everyone's lives. Can you avoid marketing and promotion through social media? Sure. Should you? No. I can see how you'd feel that way. Some people see an ocean of opportunity and get overwhelmed, while others might have had a bad experience and swore off all social media.

The fact is, quite a few of your potential readers and customers are residing on social media. If you want to get your ideal readers' attention, you need to meet them where they are. Not all readers are just hanging out on Amazon in the reviews section or forum. Quite a few of them congregate on Twitter, Facebook Groups, YouTube channels, and beyond.

Before you attack any social media marketing, you need to know your ideal reader. As covered in the previous book, *Amazon Keywords for Books*, if you try to write for everyone, you write for no one in the process. Marketing and promotion work much in the same way. If you're marketing and promoting to everyone, then you're marketing and promoting to no one.

Social media is much like a crowded bus transporting its customers from one place to the next. The bus is jammed full of people carrying a variety of conversations at a fever pitch volume. If you come onto that bus screaming about your latest book, no one is going to listen. You're simply that crazy person who got on the bus at the last stop and is trying to bum a smoke for later on. No one will make eye contact with you, and no one wants to share a seat with you.

What you need to do is find a familiar face and a group of people you can relate to. Think of them as your tribe. Once you identify commonalities in your tribe or community, you can better assimilate with the rest of them. Get comfortable and get to know people. Don't worry about selling your latest book. The most important part about leveraging social media for selling more books is to build the relationship first. Human beings buy from other human beings. Until you can build a sense of know, like, and trust with your ideal audience, nothing you say will ever matter.

John C. Maxwell once stated:

> People don't care what you know until they know that you care.

Get good at getting to know people and truly put meaning behind your interactions. Don't sweat the sales; they'll come in due time.

Once you know who your ideal reader is, identify the social media platform they most frequently visit. Sadly, no part of this book will tell you where to find your werebear shapeshifter romance readers – whether in Facebook Groups or on Reddit. This is where you're going to have to study where other readers are congregating. From there, you'll need to ask yourself:

1. Can I see myself using this social media platform consistently?

2. Will I devote myself to learning this social media space?

3. Can I put my book sales on the back burner while I build real relationships?

Once you can identify the platform you wish to work on, it's time to stake your claim and place your flag in the sand. Even though I told you to go easy on beating up people about your author brand, I don't want you to think you should be a wolf in sheep's skin. The best way to be forward about who you are and what you're about is to show it. Where do you start, and what do you need?

What You Absolutely Need on Social Media

Earlier in the book, I had you reserve all the social media handles on every platform. Remember, don't sweat using every platform right now. I'm just going to get you to use one. For now, you're going to need brand congruency. The first part of being consistent is your name, your profile picture, and your profile information. When people visit you on the various platforms, they need to know it's you and not some impostor. The best way to mitigate those issues is by getting your brand matching across every platform. Don't become overwhelmed at having all these profiles. It's not your mission to manage all of them. Just pick one for now and go with it. If you build enough presence on one platform, then you can spread out to another one in due time. For instance, I didn't focus on building much, if any presence, beyond YouTube when I first started my channel, *Self-Publishing with Dale*. My attention was solely on growing my brand there. Though I had some presence on other platforms, I was only concerned about increasing my reach on YouTube. Once I broke about 1,000 active subscribers, I started looking into other avenues without distracting me from my mission of growing on YouTube.

Take your time to grow your presence. Be patient, and don't worry if the results don't come right away. It takes time, patience, and a bit of perseverance to win in the long game. Do not expect to start selling books like a maniac just because you've been camping out in a Facebook Group every minute for the past three months. It will take a lot more engagement and interaction before people start to trust you and bring you into their inner circle.

Much like any social interaction, your approach is the perceptions others will have of you. I often think about this kid, Simon, who was in a Facebook Group of other self-publishers. Simon was a bull in a China shop. He was very opinionated, lacked any real filter, and always seemed on the verge of selling something new he discovered online.

On the opposite end of the spectrum was Ava. She was the head moderator of the same group. Though she chimed in for quite a few conversations, she always delivered excellent insights and never seemed to have an ulterior motive. Ava was simply there to put the socializing in social media. Through a conversation with a client, I'd come to find out Ava did virtual assistant work. Instantly, I remembered all her contributions to this Facebook Group and how she was incredibly giving of herself. There was instant trust in what she had to offer as a freelance assistant.

I never imagined I'd be working with her for over four years! I've driven tons of referrals and new clients her way, and her business exploded.

Now, think if my client had referred me to Simon. How would that conversation have gone? Most likely, I'd be dismissive and pass at working with him. Why? Because I'd remember how he conducted himself. He was always taking and never giving.

You, as an author, must remember every interaction on social media will have rippling effects on your career for years to come. Before you get into a spit fight, before you shill your latest affiliate product, before you beat people up with links to your website, remember to be an Ava, not a Simon.

Social Media Etiquette 101

In the early days of social media, quite a few methods worked to bolster followers and grow an online presence. Fortunately, those days have long since gone. Yet many people still believe some outdated methods work for blowing up on social media. Don't waste your time on these outdated tactics for growing your social media presence.

Follow for Follow

Gone are the days when you could use your number of social media followers to flex your clout. Is a social media following important? Yes, but does it make any difference if those followers are inactive? Absolutely! Having an arbitrary number of followers is defeating the purpose. You want to have active followers who engage in your content and posts.

One of the worst, most ineffective ways to grow on any social media platform is Follow for Follow. It's a simple quid pro quo system. Two people on social media follow each other to help fluff their numbers. The tactic would be good if only it were a legitimate relationship.

Otherwise, it's simply followers with no real engagement. The key to success in social media is engagement. Modern-day currency comes by way of engagement. If you don't see any engagement on social media, then you're spinning your wheels.

It can happen to the best of us. We see other people crushing it on Instagram, YouTube, Twitter, and more. Their follower number seems to be the key to their success. Frankly, it's much more than the number of people following them. It's all about the attention they get on their given platform. No exception!

Don't bother following someone if you don't legitimately know, like, or trust the person. You can and should expect the same of people surrounding you. No one owes you a thing on social media. You don't deserve to have a certain number of followers. Until you can prove your merit and get real engagement, you won't get real followers.

Real followers are what is going to work, so don't bother doing follow for follow tactics. Don't fall into the trappings of group followings. Follow who you like, and others will follow you if it makes sense to them.

Zero Spamming Zone

> Spam (verb) — to send irrelevant or inappropriate messages to a large number of people.

Imagine taking someone out for a date. You have the whole evening planned out, you got dressed up for the occasion, and even put on your best smell good spray. Once you pick up your date, you simply jump to the part you like best – making out! Yep, you dive in hard for that big ol' kiss despite only just meeting this person.

Can you imagine the reaction of your date? You'll probably get a weird look at a minimum. Or worse yet, you might get a violent reaction.

When it comes to life in general:

No one likes someone selling to them.

Everyone likes to feel in control of most aspects of life. We want to buy things on our terms. When we're hungry, we go to the store. When we need gas for our cars, we go to the gas station. When we take a leisurely stroll through the mall, we immediately get into defensive mode when the mall kiosk worker assaults us with their sea salts, lotions, or perfumes. Why? We weren't looking for sea salts, lotions, or perfumes, and this person has entered into our space and commanded our time and attention without permission.

Now, this isn't a punch down on mall kiosk salespeople. It's more to demonstrate how people don't like to be sold anything without prior consent or knowledge. That's why you should never go into social media with the expectations to sell books hand over fist. Outside of running paid ads through Facebook, Twitter, or more, selling your wares can be off-putting to the random person who doesn't know you on social media.

If you're going to share your book, great, but you must have context first and a reason to do it beyond getting more book sales. Additionally, you'll want to make sure it's an okay practice based on the platform. I know on Reddit, most people detest self-promotion, and it sometimes results in termination from their communities called Subreddits. You need to read the room first before ever selling anything.

Even though it might seem okay, ask yourself:

1. If I saw this post from someone I don't know, would I find it helpful?

   A. If not, don't post it.

   B. If so, prove it by posting it. Then, see what type of engagement you get.

2. Will this erode the trust people have in me?

   A. If so, then don't post it.

   B. If not, then ask a few peers their opinion about it.

Spamming seems to be the easy answer, especially if you're playing a numbers game. Maybe, just maybe, you can entice one out of every one-hundred people to buy your book. All you had to do was quickly post an offer for your book in fifty Facebook Groups. If you post in fifty groups and have a hundred people in each group who see your post, you'll have fifty people interested in checking out your book on Amazon. How likely do you think that all fifty will buy? To believe you will convert one hundred percent of your visitors is insane! Let's say you have at least one out of ten people who'll buy. Then, that means in a best-case scenario, you're looking at five people buying your book.

All the while, you made this ridiculous scene in front of hundreds of people. The other 4,995 people are privy to your ways and are more apt to tune you out the next time you spam them with your latest offer. Even worse still, you might have people who'll see your work later and pass based on their first impression of your author brand.

With spamming, just don't do it. It's a waste of valuable time, energy, and effort for everyone, including you.

Tagging People — Relevant vs. Irrelevant

This doesn't apply across all platforms, but a vast majority have a feature where you can tag other people. The process of tagging is where you link another person to your post, so their following sees your post too. In theory, tagging another person makes sense, especially if it drives more engagement. Is tagging relevant to the post, or are you simply thirsty for attention from other people and riding the coattails of someone else's hard work?

I cannot begin to tell the number of times I have had to block someone on Twitter who tags me with irrelevant tweets. Inevitably, when I visit the person's profile, I find they have few followers and focus only on selling their service. This is a one-way ticket to the block button. I don't have time for people who want to leech off the attention given to me through my hard work to drive traffic to their platform.

Worse yet is when someone tags without any prior consent, context, or reason beyond pushing their agenda. No one minds a tag if it makes sense! Much like sales, no one likes to go into that transaction without permission.

When you want to increase the relevancy of a social media post, then, by all means, invite other people to the conversation through tagging. Make sure:

- It's okay with the tagged person

- There's context

- You have an end goal in mind

I've written this many times before, and I'll write it many times after. Deliver value first and be a human being. Everything else will fall into place after that. If tagging seems fit for the conversation, then by all means, do it. Don't merely tag someone for the sake of bolstering your reach. Do it because it's going to help people.

Post Frequency

How often should you post, and does it matter? When it comes to how frequent you should post, you need to measure the effectiveness, reach, and engagement of your posts first before you ratchet up the number of times you do it. For instance, on YouTube, many experts used to spout how daily video posts were how you succeeded. After all, Pewdiepie, one of the world's most-followed YouTubers, grew his social following by posting every day for ten years. Pewdiepie is different than you and carved out a niche for himself.

Look on the other end of the spectrum with YouTuber Mark Rober. He merely posts once per month and gets millions of views, watch time minutes, and social engagement. Even though Mark doesn't post every day, he makes his monthly posts power-packed and effective.

Before you commit to posting on your preferred social media platform, study the landscape, and take note of the successful influencers:

1. What are they doing?

2. How often are they posting?

3. How is their engagement?

Can you model your post frequency based on the successful influencers? What can you do to tweak it and make it yours? You don't need to be the next Pewdiepie or Mark Rober. Just be yourself and adjust as you go according to what resonates most with your audience.

Social Media Examples

I've tried to keep this book as evergreen as possible. However, I'm sure some aspects will not remain evergreen forever, especially as popularity rises or falls based on the trending platform. Despite the dangers of sharing less evergreen content, I'm going to do it anyway because it's the concepts you need to embrace, not the exact platform.

Facebook: Ads, Groups, Business Pages, Oh My!

Over the past few years, Facebook seems to have undergone a massive public punch down. Many people would have you believe Facebook is for stuffy, old curmudgeons shouting about politics and religion. The numbers tell a different story! Billions of users use the Facebook platform daily,[1] so this doesn't equate. It reminds me of how millions of music lovers throw shade on Nickelback. Yet, the band still manages to sell millions of records, sell-out stadiums, and grow in popularity. What gives?

Facebook may not be for everyone, but one could say the same for almost all social media platforms. Billions of consumers use Facebook, so leveraging this platform is a no-brainer for authors.

The options are overwhelming at first between running ads, business pages, and groups. Where do you start, and what is most important? Many would-be experts want you to believe organic growth is dead on Facebook, but I've found that to be a half-truth.

Years ago, you could set up a Facebook business page as an author, drive a bunch of likes to the page, and reach tens of thousands of readers.

Once Facebook saw they were missing out on the money-making opportunity, they tweaked their algorithm to suppress the organic reach of Facebook Business pages. This required authors to dig deep into their pockets and run ads to build relevancy on the platform.

Sure, Facebook ads can be a viable option for growing your author brand. Still, for most indie authors, it's not an affordable and sustainable option. Once you stop spending, it's not like Facebook is going to keep delivering traffic. They shut that facet off and turn their backs to you.

What if you could still get organic reach on Facebook? What if you could reach more readers organically? It's 100% possible, but it's going to require a little upfront work.

First, you needed to start a Facebook Group yesterday. Right now, Facebook Groups are the single most effective way to market directly to your ideal readers and audience. Facebook doesn't require running ads on your posts to build awareness. If you want help in getting your Facebook Group started and growing, watch my video series on YouTube at DaleLinks.com/FacebookGroups.

Next, build awareness about your business page. Whether you do it through a post on your profile or share it in your latest book, people need to know it's there. Then, you'll have to educate your audience on the best practices. If someone is interested enough in following you, they will take the right measures to see your posts.

You could simply tell your potential followers:

> Like and follow my author page at
> Facebook.com/SelfPubWithDale. Then turn the Follow
> Settings to See First, so you don't miss out on any free
> promotions, advanced reader copies, and special deals.

Tell your reader what's in it for them and exactly what they need to do. Otherwise, they won't bother with it. You will find if you abbreviate your request and keep it as simple as possible, you'll get more results. Once you fire off a post, you're more apt to get people to see it if they're following your business profile. The tricky part is getting engagement. Without engagement, your organic reach is nil. Never fear! There are a few ways you can tip engagement in your favor:

- Create posts in bite-sized chunks. Avoid long paragraphs. Instead, break up your sentences into separate lines.

- Use emojis to grab attention. It seems silly and somewhat childish, but it's fast becoming the way to command attention on a busy platform.

- Use imagery either through a picture, GIF, or video. You get bonus points if you add captions to your video. Skip to the resources section for my recommendation for quality captioning.

- Lead with a hook. You need to command attention and only have five to six words to do it, so lead with your best stuff. Think of it as the headline of a newspaper.

- Finish with a compelling question visitors can't resist. People love to share their thoughts, so if you ask them a question or to share their thoughts, they'll most likely do that.

- Always get the last word. To make the most of your engagement, you need to respond to all comments and close with an open-ended question. This keeps the conversation going while sending signals to Facebook's algorithm about the relevance of your post.

Organic reach on Facebook isn't dead. It just requires more work. Quite a few people don't want to put in the work, or they want to throw money at the problem. If you have the discretionary expense, then go for it! However, if you don't and won't bother with it, don't be surprised if you get no engagement and no growth on this lucrative platform.

One feature you can use on a Facebook Business Page is a shop. That is a great place to showcase your catalog of books. Be sure to link out the appropriate areas on Amazon. That isn't an avenue I've fully explored myself, but it's an option worth considering.

Twitter

Do not sleep on Twitter. I discovered how much I left on the table over the past few years since taking Twitter much more seriously. Rewind to between 2014 and 2015. Twitter seemed like a link dumping ground for me. Frankly, I didn't understand all the hashtags, random conversations, and trending topics. One thing I knew for sure was authors and entrepreneurs were crushing it there. I felt, at a bare minimum, I needed to get on the platform even if to add to the white noise.

As traction grew on Twitter, I started gaining the attention of various podcasters, influencers, and businesses. I landed interviews, collaborations, and sponsorships through the platform. My network exploded tenfold due to simply being active about fifteen to twenty minutes per day.

On the platform that limits you to 280 characters, doesn't let you edit a Tweet, and is the stomping grounds for the Cancel Culture Elite, you can strike out if you aren't careful. How do you leverage this platform? What are the best practices? Is this going to yield immediate results?

The best way to leverage Twitter is simply by starting. At first, you're going to be posting tweets to an audience of no one. The first thing you need to do is find and follow anyone you know on Twitter. Scroll and engage in posts of interest to you and are relevant to your niche.

Next, browse all trending topics and hashtags. You may even have to guess your way through hashtags to see if you can find your ideal audience. Though it may seem humbling and exhausting at first, if you put just a little effort in every day on Twitter, it'll pay off in the long term.

When I'm dry on ideas about what to share, I simply find someone else's tweet, then retweet it with a comment. Post your thoughts about the tweet, throw on about two to three relevant hashtags, and fire it off.

Also, you should already have a relevant profile pic and banner art. The next thing you'll need is a pinned tweet. This is an excellent time to showcase your latest book, website, or anything that'll draw more eyes to your brand. You can simply post about your latest book and leave it alone. The nice thing about pinned tweets is you can leave it up indefinitely. As readers trickle into your Twitter profile, they'll have a reminder of who you are and what you do.

Similar to the Facebook posts, you'll want to have your tweet include a few eye-catching and search engine optimized elements:

- Lead with a hook to grab attention.

- Include those cute little emojis. Again, I know it seems silly, but it's becoming ingrained in popular culture. Those who embrace it will get attention while the rest gamble with dropping into obscurity.

- Make sure you have an image, GIF, or video. If you're promoting your book, then that's probably going to be the most fitting image. I included recommendations of free or premium image services for your book in the resources section later in the book.

Tag relevant Twitter profiles when there's context. If I have a conversation with my buddy @KWheelerBooks and I share it via Twitter, then I'm going to tag him. However, do not tag someone simply to leverage their audience to build yours. It's off-putting and, in some instances, will get you blocked by that person. I've had the displeasure of being tagged without any prior permission or context. Be selective about who you tag and why you're tagging them.

If it's a close friend, then all bets are off. Just don't go overboard like some crazed and desperate MLM salesperson trying to promote their latest income opportunity or disgusting nutritional shake. You'll turn off more people than turn them on.

Quite a few people want to know the frequency of posts. This largely depends on the time you can afford. I've known some people to tweet every hour on the hour. While some only do it once per day. If you're planning to tweet frequently, you may want to consider using an automated social media posting service. From Hootsuite to ContentStudio, you've got quite a few free and premium services to help manage social media posting without you having to camp out waiting for the right time to tweet out.

Instagram

Admittedly, I was late to the game on Instagram. This platform outwardly appears to be nothing but a collection of highly photogenic models and inspirational quotes. There's far more to Instagram than you'd think. Since it directly integrates with Facebook, it should be an avenue for you to consider if you're already on Facebook.

If you're going to break ground on this platform, here are the things you need to know:

1. You need an eye-catching image or video. Do not go with grainy, potato-quality pictures from a 1990's flip phone. It just doesn't cut the mustard.

2. Long-form video resides on their IGTV feature. If you happen to shoot a book trailer or promotional video longer than one minute, you can always add it to IGTV. The nice part is you can still showcase the first minute of content on your Instagram wall.

3. Create short or long-form text that tells a story. The point of the comment is to add context to the picture. Lead with a hook, break up paragraphs into single lines, and toss in some emojis where you see fit.

4. Hashtags are a must if you want others to discover you. You can use up to thirty hashtags on a single post. Some people believe you won't get as much organic traffic if you put hashtags in the post, so they put them in the first comment instead. I don't sweat the small stuff and just add the hashtags at the end of the text.

The key to crushing it on Instagram and getting your book exposed is through building relationships. Once it's time to promote your book or post something relevant about your book in your stories, people will take notice. Take your time. Explore relevant hashtags, follow people in your niche, and comment on posts with no intention of putting the spotlight on you.

Do not leave disingenuous comments and finish with "check out my profile" or "hey, I've got a book you should buy."

Nothing screams desperation like taking the spotlight from the original poster. If you want to do everyone a favor, drop a genuine comment, and then share the picture to your stories feature. Don't forget to tag the original poster, so they know you like their content.

LinkedIn

Gone are the days of dropping your resume and calling it a day on LinkedIn. This is no longer the stuffy business professional's social media platform. Since Microsoft acquired LinkedIn around 2016, they modeled other popular social media platforms with big-time success.

LinkedIn is great for establishing yourself as the go-to authority in your niche. You can connect with your peers and other business professionals, share your latest book, and drop some 4-1-1 on related topics.

My good friend and indie author, Professor Nez, staked his claim many years ago and stood by LinkedIn for the longest time. As the site underwent major changes, Nez won big time! Because he remained so active for so many years, he has tens of thousands of followers, and his posts get plenty of eyeballs. Nez was fortunate enough to leverage his exposure on LinkedIn to land five-figure speaking gigs based on his forte in career consultation.

Imagine that – getting paid $10,000 to speak about what you love most, just by being active on a social media platform. Well, it's entirely possible, and it's even more lucrative if you're a nonfiction author. Since LinkedIn functions as a business to business social media platform, naturally, you've got a solution to their problem.

The more active and visible you are on the platform, the more likely businesses will find you. After that, it's up to you to broker a deal. I can't promise you five-figure speaking gigs or that you'll land a traditional publishing deal. I can assure you since Microsoft owns LinkedIn, they're here to stay. Set up your profile and get started today!

*A*ccording to various online sources, over 80% of online traffic in 2021 will be video.[2] People are consuming video in mass quantities. If you aren't part of the movement, you'll be at a greater disadvantage than those who are.

I'd more recently seen an old-school self-publisher tout how he felt it was a waste of time and resources. That's easy for him to say since he's spent years building his author platform, and he had the advantage of a simpler algorithm to contend with when he began. Now, it's a different game. He's the exception to the rule and has the advantage of opting out of video. The rest of us need to scrap for the readers we want and need to retain. Video is one of the easiest and most cost-effective solutions to promoting your books and author brand.

Where you have to spend thousands of dollars simply to learn how to advertise, video doesn't require much more than whatever resources you currently have. All you need is:

- A stable internet connection

- A camera — a webcam or your mobile phone camera will do

- A microphone — again, anything readily available will do. In most instances, an onboard microphone in your PC or phone is sufficient.

- Good lighting — don't take this lightly. You can make a horrible camera look like a million bucks with the right amount of lighting. Shoot with ambient daylight if you don't have adequate lighting. If not, you can always use table lamps.

- Willingness to learn the process of creating better video

Don't worry about creating cinematic masterpieces. The whole issue people get hung up on is creating perfection. The further you can make it from perfect at first, the better. As your author presence grows and you get more funding, you can upgrade your videos. Until then, stick with what you have.

Also, don't worry about the type of video editing software. If you do use editing software, simply search up free options based on your operating system. If you're using iOS, then search up "free video editing software" on your iPhone. If you're using PC, search for "free video editing software for Windows." There are so many free options it'd be crazy for you to plunk down hundreds on software that'll merely slow down your process of marketing and promoting your book.

Outside of the previous recommendations around social media (i.e., Facebook, Twitter, Instagram, LinkedIn, etc.), consider the king of all video platforms to be YouTube and its live-streaming competitor, Twitch. Both platforms are at the forefront of online video. And, if you want to reach the most viewers you can so you can win them over as readers, then you have to leverage these avenues.

YouTube and Twitch have their share of pros and cons. While it's not my place to tell you to use one platform over the other, I want to showcase why you should consider either avenue. There's no better time than now to begin creating videos on YouTube or Twitch.

The Art of YouTube for Authors

YouTube has the benefit and direct relationship with the world's most utilized search engine in Google.[3] If you can become discoverable through Google, then you've got it made. While it's not impossible to build and grow a platform on YouTube, it will be hard at first. Once you get the hang of shooting and uploading videos on YouTube, the rest becomes more manageable.

The name of the game on YouTube is – watch time. The longer you can get viewers to consume your content on YouTube, the more discoverable your videos become. This comes with a bit of a catch, though. You need to get people to watch your video, and the barrier of entry can seem impossible. If you want YouTube to serve your video to viewers, you need to have a good thumbnail and enticing title. Once a viewer clicks on your thumbnail to view your content, the next hurdle to overcome is watch time. After they start watching your content for prolonged periods, you're in like Flynn.

A few things to take into consideration when uploading a video:

1. **Keyword selection** — use relevant keywords in your title, description, and tags.

2. **Links** — though YouTube doesn't like you sending viewers off the platform, it's still a good idea to promote your books and author website. Don't go overboard on the outbound links.

3. **Pinned comment** — engagement is key, like any other social media platform, so lead with a relevant and thought-provoking question. Then, send your viewers to a previous video of yours. It creates an endless loop once you have a backlog of videos. If

you're new to YouTube and don't have many videos, include links to your latest book or website.

4. **Encourage engagement** — in the video, encourage viewers to leave comments by asking a pertinent question. Much like what we did on Facebook, you'll want to do the same on YouTube. Get in the last word by answering every comment. This sends small signals to the YouTube algorithm and bolsters the relevance of your video.

5. **Miscellaneous engagement** – Also, consider mentioning other ways to engage, including liking, disliking, sharing, or subscribing. Just don't overload viewers with too many requests. I usually stick to one per video, and I'll load it up at the beginning or the end.

When it comes to publishing videos on YouTube, be patient! Rome wasn't built overnight, and you're going to need the flexibility to succeed on this platform. Since you're using YouTube to grow your author brand, remember to always lead with it. This simple framework has served me well:

1. Lead with the topic of the video.

2. Introduce yourself and tell people who you are and what you do. Brevity is critical here. So, you can say something like:

    A. Hey, I'm Dale L. Roberts, a bestselling author and self-publishing advocate who wants to show you how to publish books that sell.

3. Go right into your content. Don't delay. YouTube viewers tend to be a bit more impatient and want their goods without all the jib-jab.

4. As you wrap up your content, direct people to another of your videos. At first, you won't have many, if any, videos to send them. Direct them to a link in your description or your pinned comment. When I wrap up a video, I avoid closing words like "in conclusion" or "that's it." Because most viewers will leave your video right then and there. Whatever you say after those closing words will be wasted breath.

Are Book Trailers Effective?

Can a book trailer be a useful promotional piece on YouTube? Are book trailers a good way to drive more sales and build awareness of your author brand? The answer will shock you.

Yes and no.

In most instances, the old-fashioned way of promoting your publication through book trailers is antiquated. Back when online video was big, and ebooks were at the forefront of self-publishing, sure, book trailers were effective. Now, video publishing is more popular. It's going to take much more than some flashy trailer you bought from a seller on Fiverr. Will that book trailer ever work? It's certainly debatable. You could use it in paid promotions through YouTube ads or even in Facebook Ads, but you'll need to know how to use those platforms first. Also, you'll have to fork up a pretty penny just to get it in front of your target audience.

Even then, there are no guarantees. In most instances, the traditional book trailer is dead. It's tired, played out, and most people will tune it out or turn to other channels with cat videos or blooper reels. You only get one chance to make the first impression on your viewers.

To make an impact, state how you are the go-to author and wrote the premier book in your niche. How do you do that? Think outside the box. Mat Best, the author of *Thank You for My Service*, did just that. Instead of making the physical book the talking point, Best spun a humorous narrative through video. Between loud guns, scantily clad women, and over-the-top shenanigans, he nailed it when it came to stopping the scroll.

Mat Best created a highly memorable book
trailer that went viral on YouTube.

I'm not telling you to do the same thing. It won't make any sense if you're a children's book author producing a video like Mat Best. What you'll need to do is think like this:

> How can I showcase the content of my book
> in a way that commands attention?
>
> What will leave a lasting impression on casual viewers?
>
> What are a few things my ideal audience can relate
> to within a good thirty to sixty-second video?

Now, to his credit, Mat Best probably has deeper pockets than most indie authors. You might have to be resourceful. If you need any further inspiration on how little you need to create videos that take off, watch any video by comedian Gus Johnson or Caleb City. These two creators use nothing more than their camera, point, and then shoot. That's it!

As a creative entrepreneur, if you're going to create and publish a book trailer, make it worth everyone's time. Remember, if you take your time brainstorming concepts, you'll find it will be evergreen content. The longer the video is on the platform, the more views it'll get in due time. The more views and watch time a video gets, the more viewers will see it over the long haul.

If you find recording video to be overwhelming, then you may want to consider live streaming video on Twitch.

The Game of Live Video on Twitch

According to Wired.com, Twitch had over 1.5 billion watch time hours of live video in April 2020.[4] Compare this to YouTube, who merely had 461 million watch time hours of live video. Twitch is fast becoming the go-to source for live streaming video. Even though Twitch began as a live streaming platform for gamers, it quickly evolved after Amazon acquired it for nearly $1 billion.[5] Even the world's largest and most successful online retailer saw something on this platform. Still, they knew they were getting into a market that needed some more guidance to appeal to a broader audience.

Fast forward to today, and you'll find the most successful live streaming content creators are outside of the gaming realm. Scores of authors, including me, are now streaming their content on Twitch. They're doing everything from IRL (in real life) to writing sprints to book reviews and beyond. Twitch embraces and even showcases the creative entrepreneur.

There's one catch when it comes to streaming on Twitch. BYOA – bring your own audience. Despite the platform owners, Amazon, having one of the most sophisticated search engines on the market, Twitch doesn't have much of a search engine. It bases relevance on how many concurrent viewers are consuming and engaging in your content, which is just a popularity contest. As an example, you're streaming a book reading on your channel and have three viewers. At the same time, another author is streaming a book reading and has forty viewers. The Twitch search engine will serve the latter channel over your channel based on the sheer volume of active viewers.

Not to be confused, Twitch won't take away from your viewers. Still, they're less apt to add any more people to your stream based on your performance compared to other channels streaming similar content.

It would behoove you to gather as many friends, family, and fans to join you for your streams. Build as much awareness as possible for each live stream. Do not take this lightly. You must bring your own audience or face the sad music of streaming to no one. Promote your live streams on social media and send out details to your email list.

What exactly can you do to market and promote your books on Twitch? Simply being visible isn't enough to get people to buy your books. I'd recommend considering a few of these ideas to grease your creative wheels and get your live stream going:

- **Write-alongs** — this largely depends on how comfortable you are in sharing your content. You can screen share your manuscript as you type it out. If you're worried about pirates stealing your content, relax. You're essentially creating a copyright by video, and this can be admissible evidence should you need to escalate litigation.

> Fans watching get to have a sneak peek into your upcoming work. The more of a backlog you build, the more invested they'll be in your live streams.

> You get bonus points if you involve your community in the direction of your manuscript. Write-alongs are a great way to break writer's block since you have a little outside influence in the creative process.

- **Live writing sprints** — other writers might want to join you while you write. It's one of the best ways to keep you focused while working on a time crunch. I'm doing it right now with this book.

  > You can do live writing sprints two ways — with or without a screen share of the manuscript. Either way, you can always cue up a stopwatch or timer. Once the time passes, let your viewers know.

- **Advanced readings** — read your latest manuscript or segments of a book.

- **Gaming sessions** — have your followers join you for fun games. As a reward, you can gift out copies of your latest book — ebook, print book, or audiobook. It's entirely up to you. People love games and getting rewards for participating.

- **AMA** — ask me anything is a fun way for followers to get a sense of who you are.

What you stream on Twitch is only limited to your imagination. Just remember, if you want to get any real traction on this platform, you must be consistent and invite people to the party.

If you have a Twitch profile set up, interweave your books and writing through the channel graphics, including the channel art, panels, and outbound links. A great way to advertise while you stream without having the hassle of typing out the comments is with a stream bot. You can look up any number of free services that'll integrate with your live stream. I currently use StreamElements to manage my stream bot. All I had to do was add a few lines of copy, set when to release the comment, and include special considerations for posting a comment. It's way easier than you know and can be effective in passive marketing.

Most of your viewers won't even realize it's a bot. Since it's promoting your work, naturally, your viewers will be more inclined to check it out. Just remember, a little goes a long way. You don't want your bot beating up viewers in the chat every five minutes with your latest werebear shapeshifter romance novel. Have your bot post about once per hour. Put yourself in your viewers' shoes, and you'll know how much is enough.

Other Live Streaming Alternatives

Could you live stream anywhere else besides Twitch? Absolutely! It's entirely up to you on where you want to stream. Some great places to start:

- YouTube

- Facebook Live

- Periscope

- Instagram Live

- LinkedIn Live

The key to gaining any traction in live video is staying consistent. Viewers appreciate a regular schedule and full transparency. You can't expect to get great results if you stream at sporadic and unpredictable times. If you have no choice than to stream whenever life allows you then, I'd recommend promoting an email notification squad. Announce to your live audience you'll send them notifications and a schedule of live broadcasts. That way, they can join and support you for any upcoming broadcasts.

Of course, having an email notification squad is great for regular streamers too. Still, it's not as essential as it is for streamers who are not consistent. The email list can be your saving grace and a great way to get feedback from your current viewing audience.

Are you stuck on what times or days you should live stream? Then, ask your email list. It's tough to get a clear answer from your audience if you're live streaming. After all, if they're watching you, then chances are pretty likely that's a good day and time. You want to get a more overhead view of what everyone prefers.

Once you have a good idea of the best times to stream, adjust your schedule accordingly. Then, you avoid streaming to no one every time you go live. It can feel defeating enough as it is when streaming to no one. To make matters worse is when you have an audience, but no one comes to see you live.

Save yourself the heartache and start an email list for your notification squad. Then, when you go live, you can gather as a community and have a great time!

*H*ere's the part everyone inevitably skips to because it seems like the most straightforward steps in marketing and promoting a book. I implore you to visit the previous options before ever considering this avenue. Why? Because the earlier options can be free and cost way less. There's far more risk when putting your hard-earned money into paid advertising.

Clearly, this chapter will not be an exhaustive overview of Amazon Advertising. I'm going to give you enough information to be dangerous. Consider reviewing the resources in the back of the book for deeper dives into Amazon Advertising. Certainly, I don't want you to skip this chapter, because if you're new to Amazon Ads, then this is the best first steps to using the platform.

Why Amazon Advertising?

Amazon is a gigantic marketplace with billions of products. With every passing day, millions more products flood the market. It's no surprise how authors publish books only to see their titles drop into obscurity. Gone are the days when you could simply publish and pray for the best. This retail platform is hyper-competitive. Amazon Advertising is one of the best ways to be seen and heard above the noise.

Many experts will argue how Facebook Ads or Google Ads are more effective than Amazon Ads. Though Amazon Advertising is somewhat archaic compared to its predecessors, Facebook, and Google, it's come a long way over the past two years. I'd even gamble to say by the time you're reading this, the features and availability have improved immensely. Why? Amazon loves money. They don't just love the customer's money; they love your money too.

Amazon Advertising is simply another vehicle for the retailer to gather customers. Make no mistake about it, Amazon wants you to succeed. If you make money through advertising your books on their platform, then they make money. However, they're not losing anything if you dump money blindly into advertising campaigns yielding no results. They're not going to give you a polite email telling you what you're doing wrong. The amount of resources on creating better ad campaigns is embarrassingly low for Amazon.

That's why it's on you to learn this platform as you go. Quite a few would-be experts will have you believe there's a magic formula of used keywords, cost-per-click, and ad launch day that works best. All of them are wrong, but some of their information bears merit in your advertising campaigns.

For now, the best first step for any newbie is to consider what you can afford to lose. Yes, I didn't mistype that. When starting any type of advertising, you need to go in with the expectation to lose money. After all, if you've never used Amazon Advertising before, it's going to take time for you to get used to the platform. If you have experience in Google Ads or Facebook Ads, you're at a greater advantage.

Nonetheless, invest money you can stand to lose. I'll explain a more practical strategy and give you an action plan based on what works best for your budget. Rest assured, I will not recommend you spend hundreds of dollars per day. You'll be shocked at how low I recommend you set your budget. Before we dive into what to spend, it's important to know the most essential metrics.

Impressions, Clicks & Sales, Oh My!

When running an ad campaign on a book, there are three powerful metrics you have to pay the closest attention to, including:

1. Impressions — when Amazon serves your ad to a customer. If Amazon places your ad in front of a customer, then that counts as an impression. The best part about impressions — they're free.

2. Clicks — are when the browsing customer clicks on your ad to see more about your book. Clicks determine the success of your ad.

3. Sales — are the ultimate metric. When you can nail this metric, you've mastered Amazon Ads.

However, none of these metrics mean squat if you don't have a grasp on what to spend. It'd be nice if we could simply pay x-amount of dollars per month and get our ads served. It doesn't work that way. You have to go into Amazon Ads with a competitive mindset. You are vying for customers' attention, while millions of other authors are doing the same.

Determining the Cost Per Click

When you set up an ad, Amazon Advertising will ask how much you are willing to pay per click. Being a newbie, it can be overwhelming. What does a click cost? How much is a decent price to get a customer's attention? Why do you have to even guess in the first place?

First, you should never, under any circumstances, use the suggested bid feature. It's essentially like letting Amazon reach into your pocket and take what they want. In most cases, these bids are absurdly high. The return on investment will be marginal at best, and in some instances, a complete loss.

Amazon Advertising acts as a real-time auction-based system. Imagine millions of authors bidding for millions of ad placement types. Unlike any real-world auction, Amazon plays by a different set of rules. Though an auction typically favors the highest bidder, Amazon Advertising is a bit trickier. Since an algorithm runs Amazon search, the ads platform leans heavily on it for determining the most favorable outcome for the customer.

In my book, *Amazon Keyword for Books*, I discussed the complexity of the Amazon algorithm. To summarize it, Amazon favors books it deems relevant. They base algorithmic relevance on sales, product page engagement, and several other factors. The primary driving force in determining algorithmic relevance is sales. If a book sells, Amazon deems it more relevant than a book that does not drive sales. These are the cold, hard facts here, folks.

That is largely why Amazon Ads give a slight advantage to authors who use it than those who don't. Ads, in theory, build awareness and hopefully drive sales. More sales equate to more relevancy in the Amazon algorithm.

In the real-time, auction-based system, you're vying for the coveted placement in front of the customer through a specific keyword, product placement, or delivery type. You're not the only one. Others want that same spot at the very same time. Rather than give everyone a participation trophy, Amazon has to play favorites. Ad placement is an algorithmic-driven decision.

As a rough example, John and Pam publish books in the yogurt niche. John's book sells about twelve copies per day, and Pam's book sells only one copy per day. For the keyword "yogurt," John bids thirty-five cents, and Pam bids ninety-five cents. In a real-world auction, Pam would win since she bid the highest. On Amazon, the winning bid goes to the product with more relevance. Since John has a proven seller in the niche, Amazon will lean in favor of his book versus Pam's book. Pam doesn't go home empty-handed, though. Her book might still bear relevance so that she might get second servings after John. That means John's ad will get better placement, while Pam's ad will get placement after John.

Here's the cool thing. Because John won the auction, no one has to pay above that amount. Rather than spending ninety-five cents for her placement, Pam will pay under the amount John bid. Pretty cool, right? However, I've minimized a rather complex topic that does have more variables in it.

When it comes to determining your cost-per-click, see what Amazon suggests. You need to figure out what cost makes the most sense from an odds standpoint. I base a large motivating factor on how I dial in my cost-per-click on the net profit of a given book.

Here's a rough example that paints a basic picture: my book is $19.95, and the net profit is $6.97. Now I'm going to figure out what I'm willing to lose from the net profit to get a decent return on my investment. In theory, I profit $6.97 per sale of a book, so I should be able to spend up to $6.97 before I become concerned. The issue lies in how I bid. If I place a bid at $1 cost-per-click (CPC), I will only get seven clicks to get a sale and remain at the break-even point.

However, if I bid seventy cents per click, I can get up to ten clicks. I have three more opportunities to turn a profit. What if I bid only seven cents per click? Then, I could get up to one-hundred clicks to turn a profit. The issue is on the real-time auction. Bidding too low won't even get your ad served anywhere. It's almost like showing up to a formal dinner party in jean shorts and a cutoff. You won't be well-received, and most people are going to avoid you like the plague. Amazon won't serve your ad anywhere since the more relevant books are taking higher placement based on a higher bid.

There are only so many spots Amazon can offer to advertisers before they are all filled up. If you aren't speaking the same language as others are in your niche, you won't get a single impression. If you find you aren't getting many impressions, then adjust your bid upward. Only move it up slightly, and don't go overboard. Let's say you have a keyword bid at 7¢, and you aren't getting impressions. Move it up to 10¢ to 12¢ to see if that will open things up.

When starting in ads, it will take time to get a sense of what to expect and bid in your chosen niche. Don't expect to win them all. Some ads will be winners, while others are going to be duds.

If your impressions are up, then you're bidding at an optimal level. Let's say you're getting tons of impressions but no clicks. What do you do then? You have to analyze two areas:

1. **Book cover** — is your book cover as great as you think it is? Measure it up against other books in your niche. If it matches the niche, then you're good. If it sticks out like a sore thumb, then you need to change it.

2. **Relevance** — Is the keyword or product you selected relevant to your book? Even though you might think "military science fiction" is an excellent keyword for your book, that doesn't mean customers agree with you.

However, if you find you're getting clicks with no sales, then you have one of two problems:

1. **Book description** — the most significant barrier of entry in customers visiting your product page is your cover. Once they get there, you need to entice them to buy or stand to lose them. If you're getting the visitors, but not getting the sales, you've got a book description problem.

2. **Customer disconnect** — Sometimes, customers will unwittingly click an ad. In some cases, they're simply window shopping, and you get to foot the bill for their tire-kicking ways. Analyze the keyword or product choice in your ad to determine if you should keep spending money serving that audience.

Once you've gotten the impressions, the clicks, and the buys going, you shouldn't have any issues. As long as you've kept your bid at a reasonable level, you should see a return. If you don't see a return, then nix what's blowing through your daily budget. That leads me to the most crucial part of advertising – your daily budget.

Determining Your Daily Budget

This is the single most misunderstood part of advertising on Amazon. Most authors assume if they have the money, then customers will come. Unless you know what you're doing, you're essentially handing over your money to Amazon, and they won't question it.

I cannot overstate this enough, so let's repeat it for emphasis. Do not invest more than you are willing to lose in advertising. If you're new to Amazon Ads, you need to invest the money as if you're paying for an education. Don't spend it blindly or expect to learn through osmosis. You're going to need to monitor your ads daily, analyze the performance, adjust the bids, pause low-performing keywords or products, and check your search terms report. Every day you should be picking up small hints on what's working for your ad and what isn't working.

As a baseline, I'd recommend starting at a daily budget at $1 to $10 per day. I know Amazon recommends you start with $10 per day, but they don't forbid you from running at $1, so start low. Here's your new motto when it comes to advertising anywhere:

> **Start low, scale slow.**

Instead of throwing countless dollars down the drain and hoping for the best, you're going to invest your money wisely. It all starts with keeping your daily ad spend as low as you can handle for the next thirty to ninety days. If you do not have enough money to invest in ads for the next month, don't start. If you do the math behind it, at a daily ad spend of $1 per day over thirty to ninety days, you'll spend $30 to $90. On the higher end of things, at a daily ad spend of $10 per day over the same period, you'll pay $300 to $900.

For your first ads, keep your bids extremely low. You're going to make even those extreme coupon clippers and spendthrifts blush at how low you bid. While some people flex on how much money they blow on ads, you'll brag about how little you spend. I generally start with about 10¢ to 15¢ cost-per-click (CPC). Again, forget about the suggested bid and just start with a low CPC.

If you aren't seeing any impressions in the first seven days, you'll need to increase your CPC. Move up the CPC by about 2¢ to 5¢. Give it another week before you move it higher. Only move up bids on non-performing keywords. If a keyword is getting hundreds to thousands of impressions in the first week, you're on the right track.

If you see impressions and clicks, but no sales, then analyze the data first. If it's a simple case of only a few clicks and no buys, you don't have enough data to prove any statistical relevance. As an example:

- Neutral Results

  > Keyword: bow staffs for children = 1,000 impressions, 10 clicks, 0 sales

    * This is just not enough data to determine its effectiveness

- Bad Results

  > Keyword: bow staffs for kids = 1,000 impressions, 100 clicks, 0 sales

    * This keyword is a dud. If you aren't converting at least one out of a hundred clicks, then you've got a problem with the keyword selection or the book description.

- Good Results

  > Keyword: bow staffs for toddlers = 1,000 impressions, 100 clicks, 10 sales

    * This keyword is good as long as your CPC isn't too high. You're converting one out of every ten clicks, or about 10% of all customers. If you can convert at an even better rate, then you're off to the races!

It will take time for you to get an idea of what keywords perform good and bad. Then, you can pause all bad keywords and then toss them into your negative keywords as an exact match. That way, any customer searching with that given keyword will not see your ad. After all, if the keyword performs poorly, you don't want to keep paying for it.

The Research Ad

Every ad you start should begin with a research ad: a campaign that simply tests the waters. You'll want to activate a sponsored product ad and use manual keywords. You're allowed to have up to 1,000 keywords, but don't use all 1,000 slots. I used to lean heavily in filling all of the keyword slots; however, it leaves little wiggle room for you to add to a campaign that may take off. Stick with 500 to 800 keywords.

All ad campaigns have a certain amount of shelf life before they run out of steam. I've had some ads perform well for up to a year at a time while others ran well for ninety days and petered out. Sadly, I can't explain this anomaly, but you safeguard your campaign once you leave a little wiggle room.

As an ad starts, you'll see the impressions, clicks, and sales come through. Pay the closest attention to the clicks and sales. Once you see a click or sale, go to your **Search Terms** report. Find out what the customer searched for when they found your ad. If you were using a broad keyword, you'd likely see some variation of that associated with your ad.

Customer search term	Keywords	Match type	Clicks	Spend	cpc
Total 39			49	$11.75	$0.24
marion mathews	marion mathews	Exact	1	$0.09	$0.09
calisthenics dvd training	calisthenics	Phrase	1	$0.24	$0.24
foam rolling	foam rolling	Exact	1	$0.21	$0.21
women workout books	workout	Phrase	1	$0.23	$0.23
100 workouts without equipment	workouts without equipment	Phrase	1	$0.43	$0.43
aaron alexander align book	aaron alexander	Phrase	1	$0.44	$0.44
bigger leaner stronger	bigger leaner stronger	Exact	1	$0.25	$0.25
blandine calais germain	blandine calais germain	Exact	1	$0.20	$0.20
book core exercises	core exercises	Phrase	1	$0.48	$0.48
calestentics workout book	workout	Phrase	1	$0.10	$0.10
calisthenics	calisthenics	Exact	3	$0.62	$0.21

The Search Terms report shows what customers
search when they discover your book.

Using the same theory we did for determining the rough statistical relevance, we'll do the same with your search term report. Is the keyword converting into a sale? If so, copy the keyword, make a note of the CPC, add it to your campaign as an exact match, and if you're feeling bold, the phrase match. This is your way of declaring to Amazon, "I only want people who say (insert your exact keyword here) to see my ad."

With the phrase match, you're telling Amazon, "I only want people to see my ad who say (insert your phrase keyword here) with a little bit of deviation."

As a rough example, if your phrase match keyword is "paranormal romance," then the ad might be seen by customers who search:

- Paranormal romance for teens

- Shapeshifter paranormal romance

- Werebear paranormal romance for teens

Keep in mind that these are just rough examples, not an exhaustive list of all the variations related to the exact phrase match of "paranormal romance." As you can imagine, the combinations of "paranormal romance" and other words are limitless.

Now, it's natural for you to wonder - where do you get the keywords? There's a variety of ways you can do it. In my first book in this series, *Amazon Keywords for Books*, I discussed finding all the right keywords. The best way to build a list of 500 to 800 keywords is with a keyword research tool. Spending countless hours coming up with that many keywords is insane. If you want a no-cost tool, then look into Google Ads' Keyword Planner. You'll have to jump through a few hoops to secure a Google Ads account, but once you do, you should be able to use their keyword planner 100% free of charge.

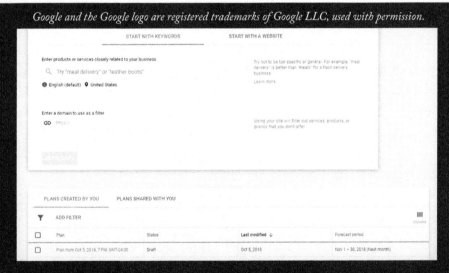

Google and the Google logo are registered trademarks of Google LLC, used with permission.

The Google Ads Keyword Planner is an excellent resource for finding plenty of keywords fast.

Simply enter a keyword into the Keyword Planner, and you'll get scores of related keywords. Download the spreadsheet. Then, copy and paste all the keywords into an Amazon Ads campaign. Before adding all the keywords, be sure to switch the setting to "Custom Bid" and set your bid low. Again, we're just doing a research ad.

Why do I start all ad campaigns for my books with a research ad? I can uncover the low hanging fruit while building relevance for my books and ads. Quite a few keywords are untapped, and no one is bidding on them. While everyone else is fighting for scraps on the competitive keywords, you can be unearthing the diamonds in the rough.

For example, when I used Publisher Rocket (see more in the resources section) for my book, *The 90-Day Home Workout Plan,* I kept getting the keyword "penis enlargement." Naturally, my book has nothing to do with male genitalia. For whatever reason, Publisher Rocket felt I needed to add "penis enlargement" to my ad campaigns. Fair enough, I thought. I finally gave in and let it go through. I started at an absurdly low bid of 8¢.

Out of the gate, I didn't get many impressions at all. I didn't see much action at all with that keyword, but once I got a click, I got a sale. That went on for months. Without fail, every time I got a click, I got a sale. We can speculate on why a customer would want my book based on that keyword, but the bottom line is it worked. What is the best part? It converted at 8¢ CPC. The net profit for every book, including the ad spend, was $6.89. Yes, "penis enlargement" wasn't what I imagined as being relevant to my book. Once I found the unusual keyword converted, I wasn't going to argue.

Now, I'm not telling you to find racy or edgy words to add to your campaigns. This story is more to illustrate a point. While most people fought for ad placement with "exercise" or "workouts" from 25¢ to $1.50, I selected more obscure keywords. My competitors spent more and profited less while I profited more while risking less. That's the ticket with research ads. You want to find the keywords no one else is using and bid low enough to get placement and convert to sales.

Once you get enough of these small victories, it adds up. Your title becomes more relevant, and when you go to battle other authors in your space for ad placement, you're more apt to win the bid without having to break the bank.

When it comes to Amazon Advertising, there are a few rules you must honor:

1. Never invest what you can't stand to lose.

2. Monitor all ads daily.

3. Adjust every campaign to mitigate any unnecessary spending.

4. When one ad dies, put another in its place.

To be clear, Amazon Advertising is not for everyone. If you aren't patient enough to learn how to use this tool, then don't. If you can't dedicate at least fifteen to thirty minutes a day to learning the system and tweaking your ads, then don't do it. However, if you have the discretionary expense, the time, and the willingness, Amazon Advertising might be for you. Again, for a more in-depth look into advertising on Amazon, visit the resources in the back of this book.

he more visible you make yourself, the more opportunities people get to know who you are and what you do. Author appearances should be integral to every author's marketing plan. If you do not currently have author appearances as part of your plan, it's time to change that.

I understand some authors don't like to be in the public eye. Some break out in hives at the thought of being seen. It's much easier than you know if you only get out of your own way and get in front of more people. Where do you start, and what do you need?

What You'll Need First — The Press Kit

For many new authors, you're going to have a tough time whipping this part together. With a little creativity and an ability to humblebrag, you can do it. Before you reach out to anyone about doing anything or appearing in any capacity, you'll need a press kit.

Your press kit should include these four things. I'll elaborate below:

1. One or two headshots

2. A short bio

3. Relevant links

4. BONUS: Media roll

The headshot needs to be professional and should not be a selfie. If you can't afford a professional photographer, then have a friend take a picture of you in a well-lit area with minimal background distractions. Do not skimp on the resolution or quality. This means your old-school flip phone won't cut it. However, if you have an iPhone 11 or any recent smartphone, you have a good camera for shooting a picture.

You should be the focal point of the shot and not the pile of dirty clothes in the background. Remember, you want people to perceive you as a professional. A little smile goes a long way, so lighten up a little bit. That is, unless you're writing dark horror suspense novels. In that case, appear brooding and troubled.

Once you have a good shot, you'll need it in two different formats. Keep one file in the original quality. Convert the next one to a PNG with a transparent background. If you're familiar with graphic design software, then this should be an easy fix. If you don't know how to do it yourself, you can outsource this task or find an online tool. Again, resources are in the back, including the services I prefer.

When it comes to your biography, keep it short and sweet. One or two hundred words will suffice. Any more is too much for your prospects to read and digest. You want short, punchy ad copy that leaves a lasting impression. Make sure you aren't covering the story of your life. Speak only about things relevant to your niche.

In my bio, I don't bother sharing what college I went to, how I grew up in a military family, or that I'm a former professional wrestler. Though my backstory is interesting in an interview, it's not the best first impression I want to make.

Next, you need to tell people where to find you. Don't go overboard. Less is more. Lead with your most important website to your least important. In some instances, having too many links will overwhelm a host. Naturally, they might select the first one and call it done. I'd recommend leading with your author website. Follow it up with any social media links. It is entirely up to you where you wish to drive traffic. Only send people to sites where you are currently active. Don't send someone to LinkedIn if you never use it. Send them to places you are active and have more examples of how awesome you are.

Save your author bio and relevant links on one document. You can do it on a standard document file or to a PDF. Dress it up on Canva or by ordering a service through Fiverr. I like to save my bio and links sheet as a document (i.e., .doc or .docx). When I need to edit, I can do those quickly without having to redo some fancy PDF. I don't sweat this area too much because the next option is where I throw in the wow factor.

The media roll is a fancy breakdown of all the things a prospect can expect from you. Remember how I told you to go easy on your bio. That's because now we're going to lay it on thick.

The media roll is a compilation of the press kit. Now you're going to include a few other pertinent talking points. Include your headshot and other pictures of you in the wild. That way, they know you aren't just some stuffy writer. Next, include your bio, any accolades or awards you earned, and your experience level. Do not take your experience level lightly. You don't need to fluff it up or dress it down. Sometimes, people are looking for a specific level of experience, so you don't want to put yourself into situations you cannot handle.

Though it's a bit daunting at first for newbies, include your social media reach. Showcase the platforms you're actively using and the followers you amassed. Include your handles and your links so people can easily access your social media platforms. Do not worry about how many followers you have. In some instances, people are more interested in how active you are and what type of engagement you get.

In an interview on the Restream YouTube channel (DaleLinks.com/RestreamInterview), the Head of Partnerships at Restream addressed a viewer question about what companies consider when finding a good fit. Her big insight was she didn't care about how many followers someone has. She only focused on community engagement. That's powerful! If you're hosting a party of a hundred people, and no one is dancing, then some prospects might pass working with you.

It's better to have a party of ten where everyone is going buck wild and having a good time. This means you're a great party host, and more people are bound to join you in due time.

Speaking of being quite the host, gather any testimonials, reviews, or positive words about you. Of course, don't fake it. If you've had an excellent review of your book or a client who raves about you, then the media roll is a place to showcase it. Three to four testimonials are sufficient, with about two to three short sentences about you.

The last step is critical to making a good first impression. You must convert your media roll into a short yet eye-catching report. For the bio and relevant links, it's okay to have a simple document, but for the media roll, you need to pull out all stops. I used Canva to create mine and did it within thirty minutes. Now and then, I update the media roll with the latest stats, which only takes me about five minutes. If you have neither the time nor patience to do it yourself, hire out. Every person I hand off my media roll to remarks on how much they liked it. You'll thank me later when you put a little time into this asset.

ABOUT ME

indie author

After plying my trade as a writer in the world of indie publishing, I decided to pay it forward and share my insights with other authors in the publishing community.

Since starting Self-Publishing with Dale on YouTube in 2016, my educational videos amassed over 1.5 million views and helped countless authors and self-publishers build a rock-solid publishing business.

39.2K
YOUTUBE
SUBSCRIBERS
Since April 2016

2K
TWITTER
FOLLOWERS
Since May 2017

4K
FACEBOOK GROUP
MEMBERS
Since June 2018

About my brand

SELF-PUBLISHING
WITH DALE

I share new content weekly on YouTube and host one live stream for self-publishers every Monday at 12pm EDT on Twitch.

In the process of growing a community on YouTube and Twitch, I've built and grown an active following of over 4,000 members in the Facebook Groups called Self-Publishing Books and the DIY Publishing Course Community.

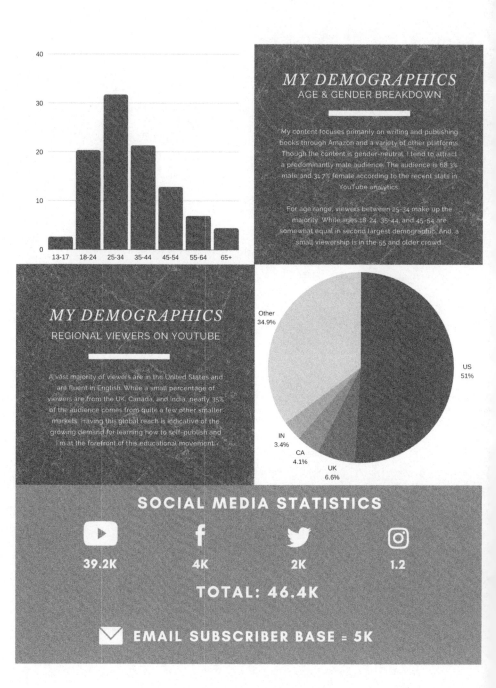

MY DEMOGRAPHICS
AGE & GENDER BREAKDOWN

My content focuses primarily on writing and publishing books through Amazon and a variety of other platforms. Though the content is gender-neutral, I tend to attract a predominantly male audience. The audience is 68.3% male and 31.7% female according to the recent stats in YouTube analytics.

For age range, viewers between 25-34 make up the majority. While ages 18-24, 35-44, and 45-54 are somewhat equal in second largest demographic. And a small viewership is in the 55 and older crowd.

MY DEMOGRAPHICS
REGIONAL VIEWERS ON YOUTUBE

A vast majority of viewers are in the United States and are fluent in English. While a small percentage of viewers are from the UK, Canada, and India, nearly 35% of the audience comes from quite a few other smaller markets. Having this global reach is indicative of the growing demand for learning how to self-publish and I'm at the forefront of this educational movement.

Other 34.9%
US 51%
IN 3.4%
CA 4.1%
UK 6.6%

SOCIAL MEDIA STATISTICS

39.2K   4K   2K   1.2

TOTAL: 46.4K

EMAIL SUBSCRIBER BASE = 5K

DALE L. ROBERTS

SELF-PUBLISHING EXPERT &
VIDEO CONTENT CREATOR

CONTACT DALE

614-555-5555
dale@selfpublishingwithdale.com
www.selfpublishingwithdale.com

 youtube.com/selfpublishingwithdale

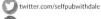 twitter.com/selfpubwithdale

 facebook.com/selfpubwithdale

instagram.com/selfpubwithdale

YOUTUBE STATS AT A GLANCE

MONTHLY AVERAGE
Views: 93.1k
Watch time minutes: 497.8k
Audience growth: 1.5k

TOTAL
Views: 2.1m
Watch time minutes: 10.8m
Subscribers: 39.2k

SEE WHAT OTHERS SAY ABOUT DALE...

"The best thing to happen to my self-publishing business was stumbling onto Dale's YouTube channel."
-Moninque "Mojo" Siedlak, indie author

"His straight to the point approach is appreciated and has an in-depth knowledge of the industry few offer."
-Darrin Wiggins, indie publisher

"Although I've been publishing books in Amazon since 2011, I found Dale's YouTube channel over a year ago and immediately recognized his great talent: not only as an expert self-publisher but also as teacher and communicator."
-Alvaro Parra Pinto, YouTube Video Creator & Indie Author

"Dale has been called a guru, a label that I know he dislikes, but in my self-publishing business he is simply my mentor and friend."
-Mark Brownless, Indie Author

"Dale L. Roberts is an amazing, generous and helpful person who has a true knowledge of the publishing business."
-Anna Nadler, Indie Publisher

You will not have to invest a ton of money. In fact, I wouldn't recommend investing much, if any, money at all. I'm a spendthrift at heart and recommend using free resources like Canva or GIMP to get the job done. When push comes to shove, and you're short on time or energy, outsource!

The last vital step in the press kit assembly is uploading to a cloud drive. You'll want to store all your items in one folder with a shareable link. With that shareable link, create a short link. Bitly has a free service for link shortening. Even better, WordPress has a free plugin called Pretty Links. It essentially creates a subdirectory on your own domain that redirects to the shareable link you created. If you don't have WordPress, but own a domain name, visit your domain name service provider, and ask them to set you up with a subdomain that redirects to your given link. Most services provide unlimited subdomains at no extra cost.

Examples:

1. Bitly Link — bit.ly/bookreview

2. Subdirectory — dalelinks.com/**marketingbook**

3. Subdomain — **marketingbook**.dalelinks.com

Whatever you do, avoid sending the full, unedited link. It reeks of amateur hour, and it's also not something a prospect will easily remember later. It's easier to remember your author-specific website or bitly link.

Media Appearances

Under the media appearances umbrella, we're going to focus on various ways you can reach your audience. It's not solely limited to being on television or getting a YouTube channel for an interview. We'll find a host of options that will benefit your author brand

To clarify, media appearances on their own will not sell a ton of books. The process of landing media appearances can seem overwhelming, and your ego may take a hit when you see your book sales don't move much. That's okay because we're focusing on the long-term goal. Appearing in front of as many people as possible builds awareness of who you are and what you do. It takes up to eight interactions with any one person before you develop a sense of trust.[6]

Chances are likely if you're appearing on the local morning show, viewers are seeing you for the first time. Naturally, you'll think the interview went well, and your interviewers might even remark on how well you did. The reality is it's going to take much more than a single appearance on a morning show before anyone will rush to buy your book. Sure, there are exceptions to the rule. For the vast majority of us, it's a grind.

You might wonder why even bother if it doesn't sell any books? The best analogy goes like this:

> How do you eat an elephant?

Looking at the next five years, you might feel overwhelmed having to slug out tons of interviews just to sell a few books. Sadly, it's part of the process of getting your name out there. Try to do interviews. Rather than trying to do a ton of appearances all at once, do some slowly over the long term.

Imagine if you did one appearance per week for one year. You will have fifty-two different contact points where strangers acclimated to who you are and what you do. Now, add up fifty-two weeks over the next five years, and you've got 260 different contact points. Wow! So...

> How do you eat an elephant? One bite at a time!

It's not sexy, and it doesn't make for the best plan in getting rich quick. Still, it certainly beats the alternative of investing thousands of dollars into ads that may or may not perform the way you like. Let's face it; you can control elements when landing media appearances. You can answer questions in a live interview or write a guest blog post for a website. You can't control paid advertising as well. There are so many intricate elements involved, not to mention the volatility of advertising if you're new to the game.

Media appearances require much less money and a little more time to get going. If you have more time than money, then landing media appearances is for you. The good news is if you already have a press kit, then you've already done a fair chunk of the work. Now, it's a case of sticking your neck out in a few places and seeing if you can get things going.

Where do you start, and what are the best opportunities out there? Here's a short list to consider for media appearances:

- Local television

- YouTube video interviews

- Podcast interviews

- Local libraries

- In-store appearances

- Guest blog posts

Local Television Appearances

I'll make no qualms in sharing that I've yet to make a single television appearance outside of my time in professional wrestling. It's not an area I actively pursue since my wheelhouse is in online appearances; however, I know my share of authors who have this nailed. The steps are fairly simple in landing a local television appearance.

It may not seem very savvy or as detailed as you would think, but it consists of asking. Call your local TV station and see who you have to speak to for sharing your area of expertise. Make sure you're framing it in a way that makes sense for them while showcasing your expertise as an author. A publicist for traditional publishing authors, Jason Jones, covers the exact steps you'll want to do to land appearances. Rather than misleading you, I'll send you his way so you can nail it every time. Check the resources in the back.

Written Media Appearances

Also, I discovered a really neat resource while reading a book by Honoree Corder. She recommended a news aggregate source called Help a Reporter Out. Also known as HARO, this email newsletter sends out an email three times a day with various news sources looking for specific types of content. The biggest issue is you'll have to do a lot of sifting to find a piece that fits. The easiest way to get to what you're looking for is by using a quick keyword search. Press **CTRL, F**, then type a keyword in the search bar on my computer. If it pulls up any results, then you can skip right to it. If you get no results, then simply toss out the email.

The key with HARO is getting on top of the opportunities right away. Some news sources look immediately for content, so you can't put a pin in it and hope to come back to it later. Typically, I'll let my emails pile up for one day, and then access them the next day. That way, I can peel through each email fast.

Next, you'll have to reach out to the listed contact on HARO and stay on the topic according to their request. Be brief, remain professional, and be ready for rejection. That rejection comes by way of hearing nothing at all or getting a rejection. In most instances, you'll get silence.

This situation is where having your press kit readily available comes in handy. If you spend a little time every day on HARO, you just might get an opportunity in due time. Take note of how you communicated and even ask the reporter what interested them most after fulfilling the commitment.

Online Author Interviews

This is my wheelhouse and an area I can confidently point you. If you're the type of person who doesn't want to be bothered with leaving your house, this option is for you. As long as you have an internet connection, a camera, and a microphone, you're good to go!

You aren't merely limited to any one avenue. Author interviews come in a few different formats, including:

- Video interviews

- Podcast interviews

- Website Interviews

Video Interviews

As shared previously, video marketing should be an integral part of any marketing plan. The nice thing is that even if you're strapped for time and don't have all the resources, you can always rely on someone else to do it all for you. Here is where online author interviews come in. How you land a video interview can be somewhat tricky and a bit time-consuming.

Remember how I had you set up all those social media accounts? It's now time to put them to work. Go to your preferred social media platform where video is available (i.e., YouTube, Facebook, Instagram). Search for content relevant to your niche. You want to scope out video content creators who specifically do interviews on their channel. Though it won't hurt to check out other creators, we want to zero in on video creators who interview guests.

Now comes the grind. You must watch the content. No, you don't have to view twelve hours of video content, but it's a good idea to see if you like the person's content. Otherwise, landing an interview on that channel will be an uphill battle with a terrible payoff. You need to first resonate with the content before ever considering a guest spot with the video creator.

Next, you'll want to engage in the comments with the community. Don't force it and avoid shamelessly self-promoting. Even indirect plugs will get you a side look if you aren't careful. That means, "I just got done writing my book called XYZ, and boy, am I tired."

Nope! That indirect promotion will often immediately flag you as someone with an agenda. Keep the comments and communication professional while on-topic. If someone asks you about your content, then be brief and steer the conversation back on-topic. Your primary focus is to be visible and make friends. Become part of the community and engage in meaningful ways.

You don't need to spend the next five years doing this. Still, it's generally a good idea to hang around for a couple of weeks before assaulting the video creator with your proposition. That is where many authors and entrepreneurs get it wrong with me when wanting to land an interview. I turn down more interviews than I accept because some people are not active in my community. None of my followers are invested in the guest and care less about who they are. I'm more apt to work with someone my community already knows, likes, and trusts.

Take your time, and don't rush this step. You'll know when it's the right time to take the next step. Often, a video creator will openly engage with you and even share how much they appreciate your contributions. Don't wait for an invitation to the next step.

You'll need to do a little recon once you feel comfortable with the video creator's content. Look up their website, social media account, or any of their profiles. You're looking for an email or contact form. Once you find it, reach out to them, but keep it brief. Bear in mind, video creators are busy, and answering every last message becomes an exhausting process, so keep it short. For example:

Hey, Dale,

I've enjoyed your YouTube channel for the past few weeks.

You may have noticed me in the comments from time to time.

I loved your interview with Dave Chesson; it was highly informative.

I'm reaching out to you to see how I could get an interview on your channel.

I'm a self-published author who grew an advanced reader copy team to over 1000 members in the past 90 days.

I believe your audience will love some of the insights I have.

Also, I will promote my appearance through my email list and Twitter for the next few weeks.

Thoughts?

Before you consider typing that out word for word, I encourage you to write your own. It doesn't need to be perfect. In fact, don't make it a form letter. Trust me, video creators get a ton of queries, and we know when someone has merely copied and pasted some form letter. It took me two minutes to write. It should take you the same amount of time, especially if you already know, like, and trust the creator.

Four elements to consider when approaching a video creator for an interview are:

1. **Confirmation** — Tell the creator about how you know them. Don't go over the top.

2. **Compliment** — Okay, I'm not asking you to kiss their ass, but it's a good idea to tell them why you dig their content. It could be a specific video or two, or you can even refer to something unique to the community.

3. **Deliver value** — How can you be of service to the creator's community? Most video creators want to know you have their community's best interests at heart.

4. **Quid pro quo** — Remember, you're dipping into somebody else's community they have taken the time to grow and nurture. Not

to mention, the video creator will have to work to put your interview together and promote it to their following. What's in it for them? No matter how big or small, explain to them how you plan to promote it and what audience you'll bring to the table.

If a video creator accepts your offer, honor their time by asking for a scheduling app if they have it. If they don't, be prepared to do a little schedule tag with them to make it work. I'd recommend getting a scheduling app that integrates with your preferred online calendar. Then, you can always save heartache for both of you and drop a link to it.

Remember the press kit I had you put together? It's time to put that to use. Once you get booked for a video interview, give them the press kit. Do not wait for them to ask for it. A prepared guest leaves an excellent first impression, so send that press kit right after they agree to have you on their show.

Now, find out the answer to these questions:

1. Where do you need to be?

2. What do you need for the interview?

3. How long will the interview be?

4. What expectations do they have of you?

5. Are you able to share your book and relevant links?

For any interview, I'd recommend having everything set up well in advance. Make sure wherever you plan to conduct the interview (i.e., your house, office, etc.), your background is clutter and distraction-free. No cringe-inducing virtual greenscreens! It's an awful look and will hinder more than help you. Clean up your area for the interview and be done with it.

Also, test your computer on a video chat ahead of time. Reach out to a friend and see if they'll do a video with you. Heck, it might even be a good time for you first-timers to do a mock interview. It will break up your nerves and get you relaxed for the actual interview. Watch out for glitchy video, choppy audio, or any imperfections that'll take away from your spotlight.

There are two things you must not do without in video interviews:

1. Headphones to isolate sound and avoid echoes.

2. Direct internet access — do not rely on WiFi. Avoid it at all costs. Only use WiFi if you must. It's a good idea to fully disclose with your host that you have to rely on WiFi (if you do).

Once the day comes, loosen up and have fun. After the interview, take a moment to thank the host. Do not disconnect right away, because sometimes the host might have additional points to communicate. In some instances, they might have special thanks or compliments.

Send a follow-up email thanking them for the interview. A little goes a long way. As a video creator, I'm more apt to bring someone back who was not only a good guest but went the extra distance to say thanks while promoting the content. Speaking of content, find out the interview link so you can uphold your end of the deal for promotion.

Podcast Interviews

Audio blew up big time over the past few years. Between podcasts and downloadable audiobooks, more people gravitate toward audio than ever before. Why? It's easily consumable information, you don't need much of an internet connection to listen, and it's highly accessible and portable content. Getting podcast interviews is a solid win for building awareness of your author brand.

Podcasts work much in the same way video interviews do. Most of the time, you won't even need video. Everything you did for preparation in the video arena, you can now do with audio. Before you do solicit an interview, double-check the host. Some podcasts do audio and video. You don't want to show up on the day of your interview to find out you needed your webcam on. Worse yet, imagine showing up in nothing but your underwear only to find you need to be on-camera.

I've found podcast interviews to be the easiest to land. No matter how big or small, give a podcast a shot. Don't make the same mistake I made. Quite a few times, I accepted interviews without first listening to the podcast, and it's been a comedy of errors. Some hosts are hard to understand due to thick accents or bad audio gear. Other times, the host seems more interested in pushing their content versus interviewing me.

On one podcast, I had the host do an entire intro and talk for quite a while before she ever got to me. Once the host did ask me questions, she interrupted me mid-sentence to interject her thoughts. At the end of the interview, the host wanted me to ask her questions. Yep, you didn't read that wrong; the host wanted me to interview her on *her* show. After twenty minutes of this train wreck of a podcast, I was ready to crawl in a hole and cry myself to sleep. She seemed to love my interview. I listened back and discovered it was as bad as I thought it would be. Sadly, she wanted me back, and I had to politely decline.

The moral of the story is to never accept a podcast booking without first knowing the type of content and how the host conducts the show. Had I listened to the offending podcaster's content, I would have discovered she had a history of mistreating her guests.

After any interview, whether audio or video, ask how the host felt about your performance. You aren't fishing for compliments so much as you're setting yourself up for future interviews. If the host enjoyed your content, ask them if they know of any other platforms where you can get interviews. This is a great way to get referrals! I've had some guests on my channel who knocked the ball out of the park, so I referred them to other peers in my industry. In turn, that guest got more bookings!

If your interview was horrible (and you'll know), don't approach the host about referrals. It's generally not a good look. Again, you'll know whether you did well or not. It's a gut feeling.

For getting podcast interviews, you jump through the same hoops as finding the various platforms relevant to your niche. I don't necessarily feel you should pay an exorbitant fee to a podcasting interview curation service. It's ridiculous that someone would charge a client hundreds of dollars to get on a podcast when all you have to do is lay the groundwork and do the outreach and show up.

A good free service is through a website called PodcastGuests.com. Though they have a premium service for hosting guest profiles, you'll get your money's worth through the free service alone. Every week, PodcastGuests.com sends out an email showcasing podcast guests and podcasts looking for guests. I easily landed a dozen interviews and developed long-lasting relationships with podcasters using this free service. Not every newsletter will bring back something for you, but if you keep an eye on it, it will pay off.

Website Interviews

Getting website interviews is possibly the easiest way while showcasing your skills as a writer. I tripped over this option quite some time ago when first getting into the business. How it works is the website has a form you fill out. You answer questions based on your experience and submit all your relevant information. The website then showcases you in the online interview.

It's a nice way to share who you are in a different place than your website or Amazon. The best part is this option comes 100% free. I've never found a site that charges for it. One site that's a great example of website interviews is AwesomeGang.com. It'll take you about fifteen to twenty minutes to complete.

If you're wondering where else to find author interviews like this, I'd recommend looking into promotional websites. Most want you to complete an interview because it helps them build more relevancy in search engines, especially if you send traffic to read your interview. You'd be doing yourself a great service by promoting your interview after the site posts it.

Local libraries

Not too long ago, my wife and I attended the Dayton Book Expo. We saw many great exhibitors and authors at the conference and were pleasantly surprised by a panel of guest experts. These folks were on the inside when it comes to leveraging libraries for your author brand. I never thought about working with local libraries, and according to the panelists, it is a highly untapped market.

You would be surprised to know local libraries are looking for home-grown authors to showcase in the community. The only catch is you have to be willing to put in the work and build relationships with the library staff.

Do you want to get your book into the local library? Then, speak to the branch library manager. Don't just assault them with your books and leave. You need to be willing to invest a bit more time and value to get something in return from the library. You might want to volunteer time, organize a book club, or run a workshop based on your niche at the library. All it takes is speaking with the library staff and see what you can do to help.

Landing a library speaking gig is as simple as stepping outside your comfort zone and speaking with the staff. I spoke with one panelist about her extensive experience in working with libraries. She assured me all it requires is a little time, research, and work to build a relationship with the libraries. After giving back to your community, they're more apt to have you make appearances and promote those appearances.

In-Store Appearances

Much like libraries, landing in-store appearances requires a little upfront work and patience. You'll need to visit the local bookstores and let them know who you are and what you do. Sadly, most brick and mortar stores aren't looking for volunteers. Still, if you're a regular patron who chops it up with the staff, then they'll be more receptive when you pitch an in-store appearance. The most important thing when it comes to landing an in-store appearance is WIIFT – what's in it for them?

I hate to say this, and it's not to discourage you, but authors are a dime a dozen. What do you bring to the table that all the others don't? How do you plan to advertise the appearance? What kind of foot traffic will you bring?

There's nothing sadder than the lonely author sitting at their booth in the local mom and pop bookstore. If there's no one visiting, what do you think the initial reaction will be for people? It will most likely be a dismissive reaction, or in some cases, the author might appear to be a store worker.

I'd recommend before you pitch a local store about an in-store appearance, have a strategy in place. What will you do that isn't just about signing books and kissing babies? How will you make this a memorable event? Consider developing creative out-of-the-box ideas. Instead of doing autograph sessions, maybe consider doing a read-along, a workshop, or a Q&A session. There are no limitations.

Remember to go in with a pitch that isn't just, "Hi, I'm a local author. You should host an author signing because I'm going to be big."

That won't cut the mustard, and most people will pass.

A long time ago, I was a reckless driver who had no common sense or driver's etiquette. Heck, I was so arrogant, I believed having an insurance policy was for suckers. Despite it being an Ohio mandate, I still didn't have insurance. Inevitably, I got in a wreck. Yes, it was 100% my fault. To spare you the details, I gently t-boned a car I didn't see while making a left turn in a parking lot. Thankfully, no one was hurt, but my bank account would be when it was all said and done.

Even though I hardly tapped the other car, it was enough to do damage. It was hundreds of dollars I couldn't afford. I could have avoided all of that had I shelved my ego and invested in a good insurance policy. The accident was enough to humble me, and I never did it again.

There are real-world examples in self-publishing of authors who've been just as reckless with their business. They rely solely on Amazon to build their business. These authors can pull in a substantial income only for Amazon to shut them out. The fact is, Amazon doesn't need to have a reason to terminate accounts. It's their sandbox; we're merely playing in it.

What happens when Amazon kicks you off their platform? Do you simply tuck tail and go away, or do you fight back and reinstate your account? Can't you just start a new account with a different business entity? Well, that's certainly debatable and nothing I'd recommend.

If Amazon boots you off their platform, then it's up to you to pick up the pieces and make the most of the situation.

Author terminations on the Amazon platform don't happen often, but it's still a real possibility. Much like my chances of getting into a car accident didn't seem likely, it still happened, nonetheless. Rather than thinking, "it won't happen to me," you should always prepare for the worst while expecting the best. Enter email marketing.

Email marketing is your insurance policy. The fact of the matter is Amazon has customers. You're using Amazon's platform to reach their customers. Once Amazon banishes you, you can't take the customers with you, or can you?

Well, there's a good reason why email marketing is your safeguard. By having readers join an email list, you convert Amazon customers into your followers. Once they join your email list, you have essentially brought your following with you. Now, would you have the same reach as you do on Amazon? No, but something is better than nothing. You can build a presence online through avenues like social media or a website. However, nothing compares to the relationships you create through the email inbox.

I purposely saved email marketing for the end of the book. Without any of the previous suggestions, building an email list will be an uphill battle. To get the most from building an email following, it's a good idea to:

1. Have a website.

2. Build a presence on social media.

3. Publish or plan to publish a book.

4. Understand basic marketing and promotion.

Getting someone to trust you enough to part ways with their email address is a tight rope walk. On the one hand, you've got to deliver value for them to trust you enough. On the other hand, if you over-deliver, potential subscribers will see you as a try-hard or someone who's simply in it to sell things. Sure, you want to deliver value, but in the same instance, you don't want to go overboard and scare people away. Part of that is understanding what your audience wants before ever starting an email list.

What is the Best Email Marketing Service?

Before you start gathering emails and blindly sending them out through your Hotmail account, you need to understand a few things. Never under any circumstance, do email marketing through a regular email account. It's a surefire way to get marked as spam and blacklisted online. Next, you should never send content without consent from the email recipient. You can't prove whether they consented if you simply add their email to your list. They need to opt into your email newsletter, not you. Last, you need to get a good overhead view of what email marketing is and how to leverage it.

The best place to start when it comes to email marketing is through an email service provider. You've got a ton of services to choose including:

- Mailchimp

- MailerLite

- ConvertKit

- GetResponse

- Aweber

- Infusionsoft

- And, so much more

Rather than point you to one over the other, I'll leave it up to you to research your options. If you're new to self-publishing, I'd recommend considering any service that'll allow you free services with a cap or a trial. Keep in mind, sometimes free services come with limitations, but you'll at least have an option you can use until you get the hang of email marketing.

Some services like Mailchimp and MailerLite allow up to 1000 subscribers for free. Once you have that many subscribers, you should have a good sense of monetizing your email list. You can do that by sending unique offers, announce book launches, or even build up awareness of your existing catalog.

Ask around in your community and see what your peers prefer. Take any recommendations with a grain of salt. At the end of the day, you're going to be the person in charge of email marketing, not them. If you are using an email service provider with astronomical rates, that's on you, not your friend, who recommended it to you.

Once you set up your service, you'll need to get familiar with all the tools and functions. Since all platforms have different layouts, I'll skip telling you how to get them set up. Ask yourself these questions:

- Can readers easily join the email list?

- Are the metrics easily accessible?

- What do you have to pay based on the number of subscribers and outbound emails?

In 2015, I joined several Facebook groups with successful self-publishers. Quite a few of them had me believe my email marketing efforts were futile. After all, they boasted hundreds of thousands of subscribers, and here I was with a whopping one hundred. It was rather frustrating, to say the least. What I came to understand was that the people who flexed their subscriber base were most often the ones who did nothing with that list.

They hadn't sent a single email broadcast to their subscribers. That means they didn't even give their subscribers a reason to unsubscribe. These try-hards were so busy bragging about their large base they forgot to communicate with them altogether. That's the most critical aspect of building your list. Whether big or small, always communicate regularly with your subscribers.

Understanding the Email Metrics

The point of building a list is to communicate with your audience and nurture a long-lasting relationship. Furthermore, you're building an email list so that you can sell more books, products, or services as an author. Before you can ever expect to sell anything, you need to understand what numbers are important.

With any email service provider (ESP), you will need to track opens and clicks. How many people received your email? How many of those recipients opened the email? Of those emails opened, how many people clicked on a link or offer?

Yes, having a deep list of subscribers is great, but if no one is opening your email, you've got a problem. The first barrier of entry when it comes to mastering email marketing is the subject line. You need to compel an email subscriber to open your email. That requires a bit of copywriting finesse. If you aren't good at it, don't sweat it. You can always experiment with different titles and subject lines to see what gets the best results. Some ESPs allow for split testing to try a different subject line for two groups of email subscribers. Once you find a good subject line, you can use it again or tweak it for future campaigns.

After you get the email subscriber to open your email, the next mission is to deliver value. Create an email worth reading; otherwise, they will unsubscribe or tune out all future emails. Rather than writing long-form emails, go into it with a game plan with short-form ad copy. Create a concise email with the intent to drive the traffic elsewhere. How do you do that? Simply through a link.

That brings us to the second most important metric – clicks. Where email opens get someone into your newsletter, the click sends them out of their inbox and into the online ethos. You could send them to your social media profile, a blog article, or even your latest book. The hard part is figuring out how you do it. No, you don't need special neurolinguistic programming skills or Jedi mind tricks. Again, it comes down to delivering enough value and building enough intrigue to merit a visit to your link.

After that, all bets are off. What happens next will depend largely on where you're sending them—some ESPs track sales for some sites. Sadly, there isn't any ESP who integrates with Amazon, so you won't be able to know who bought your book. That's including the use of Amazon Associates. Sadly, it's against Amazon Associates' policies to use affiliate links in emails. Instead, send email subscribers to your website since you can embed offers there.

Closely monitor how many subscribers you have, how many open your emails, and how many are clicking your links. The rest will fall into place as it should. Check the resources section for my recommended reads on email marketing. Rather than spend a lot of time lingering on email marketing, let's focus on how to get email subscribers?

How to Build an Email List

Getting an email subscriber isn't easy, but the process can be simple. Once you settle on an email service provider, you should be able to build a landing page. Most ESPs have the option to build a webpage specifically for subscribing to your newsletter. This is called a landing page or squeeze page. Most landing pages consist of a simple graphic, some ad copy, one or two text boxes for the person's name and email, and an opt-in button.

Once you create a landing page, get the URL associated with the landing page. The first thing you should do is create a short link, sub-domain, or subdirectory as a redirect. It's hard enough to ask readers to subscribe to you. Imagine how much more of an ask it is for you to require them to remember or trust a random website link.

One additional item to consider is the lead magnet, a special bonus that entices people to join your email list. Is a lead magnet required? No, but it certainly helps attract more subscribers than if you offer nothing. There's something to be said, though, about the people who subscribed with no real bribe. I've found email lists where I had no offer have the greatest open and click rate. Why? Possibly because those subscribers are more invested and loyal to my author brand and didn't need any coaxing to get onboard.

The best-performing lead magnets are sometimes the simplest to create. Don't go overboard and test out a few different lead magnets over time. Once you find an irresistible offer, drive more traffic to it. A few examples of some lead magnets you can create are:

1. **Fiction** — short story or novella — don't give away everything as a fiction author. Think about building a prequel or spinoff to your flagship books.

2. **Nonfiction** — checklist, toolkit, or mini-course — as a nonfiction author, all three perform well. In my experience, checklists and toolkits perform the best. Keep it to one page. You can even use the ever-reliable Canva to create a robust PDF download for your subscribers.

Once you have a great lead magnet, you can host it on your ESP or in the cloud. I've had quite a few files hosted in the free Google Drive service associated with my private email. I simply grab a shareable link, then paste the link in the welcome email. Once someone subscribes, the first email is the welcome email with instructions on downloading their free offer. Don't be surprised when you see this email gets the most opens and clicks. The second email or so tend to get the most unsubscribes. That's okay! That just means you can communicate directly with the people who are genuinely interested in you as an author.

The next step is to promote your landing page. You'll want to plaster this web address anywhere and everywhere, including:

- Books

- Video mentions and descriptions

- During interviews

- Your social media profile or feed

- Guest blog posts

When it comes to books, you'll want to insert the offer to join your email list in two high traffic areas – in your front matter and back matter. Anyone browsing the Amazon marketplace can see the first 10% of your book. Part of that first 10% could include a one page mention of your email newsletter. You can keep it simple with something like:

> Would you like to get exclusive offers, free advanced copies, and special discounts on books by this author? Then, subscribe at XYZ.com to join our email reader club.

Though this isn't the most effective ad copy out there, it's roped me in a few hundred subscribers in any given year. Just imagine if I added an offer they couldn't refuse. Try this:

> Wanna know the secret to sell more books with only a few minor tweaks in your publishing process? Then, download a copy of the Bestseller Book Launch Checklist today when you join the VIP Readers Club at DaleLinks.com/Checklist.

The only wrong way to build an email list is if you outright lie to get them on your list. Avoid roping in unsuspecting subscribers with outrageous claims or unrealistic promises. If you're promising to deliver three epic-length novels, then you better deliver, or you are going to have many unhappy subscribers and an eroded reputation.

Building an Advanced Reader Copy Team

To set your next publication up for the best possible success, you need to get enough hype behind the launch. Though the email list is a great place to tap into, you're going to need a narrower subset of people.

These are readers who enjoy your content and are willing to provide reviews upon launching. Enter the advanced reader copy team, also known as an ARC team.

Before you launch a book to the public, it's a good idea to build hype in your community. You can further build hype by opening up free, yet limited, access to your book to a select number of readers. The best way to find an ARC reader is through your email newsletter. You can send out a handful of emails searching for subscribers who are the most interested in receiving an advanced copy.

To make it even easier on yourself, you can simply narrow your audience in your ESP dashboard. Find out who your most engaged users are. Once you identify the group of super active subscribers, you're going to send them an exclusive offer to join your advanced reader copy team.

The ARC team members' only responsibilities are to read the book and send any feedback to you before it launches. Once the book launches, they post a review on Amazon, Goodreads, or any other platform you wish. Remember, you can't require leaving a review of your book. Amazon Community Guidelines forbid coercion or review exchanges. You can only request that they leave an honest review once the book launches. That's it.

In my Bestseller Book Launch Checklist (available at DaleLinks.com/Checklist), one of the first, most vital steps to a stellar book launch is assembling an ARC team. One of the next steps is to create a preorder followed by launching the print version of the book two weeks before the ebook launch. This release strategy allows for your ARC readers to post a review on the book before the full release of the ebook. Having reviews before the launch, you build more relevancy for your book and assist browsing customers in making an informed purchase.

Just how many members do you need on your ARC team? That largely depends on how many free copies you want to distribute. If some of your followers already read your book, then how likely are they to purchase a copy post-launch? Possibly not very likely, but it's a chance worth taking if you can get reviews on your book.

I found an ARC team is great in theory, but in practice, it doesn't always play out as planned. For instance, you might have ten members on your ARC team, but only three people post a review after launch. This means you have a 30% conversion rate of readers to reviewers. This is an actual number I had at one point. Rather than face having only three reviews on launch day, I tripled the number of team members. When I had thirty members on my ARC team, I received ten reviews post-launch. Do you see how that works? It's a numbers game. If you've done a good job in delivering a stellar publication and communicating your needs, then your ARC readers should deliver when the time is right.

I find following up with ARC team members before launch is critical. I check in to see how the reading is coming. Then, I send out an email a week before the launch, and I do it one more time on the day of the launch. If you find some ARC members are dragging their feet, follow up with them about one to four weeks after launch. Beyond that, if your ARC member isn't reading the book or posting a review, simply remove them from the team and move on.

Back in the day, I uploaded all my ebook files (epub, mobi, and PDF) to a cloud drive. Now, there are a ton of services that'll do it for you. Some services will even watermark your files and only allow for downloads after a reader jumps through some hoops to get on your ARC team. Services like BookFunnel, BookSprout, Prolific Works, and Hidden Gems Books are examples of premium sites that help with file management and gathering ARC team members.

If you're a bit more cash-strapped and want free alternatives, look into StoryOrigin or FiveABook. Both services are new on the market and are currently offering free submissions. They have a variety of services available beyond ARC building features. The one I worked with on the previous book in this series, *Amazon Keywords for Books*, was StoryOrigin. The user interface is intuitive, and the process of accepting ARC readers is stress-free.

All I had to do was upload the ebook in three formats under 7MB and three sample versions of each file type. If you're having issues with getting the various file types or compressing your files, the team at StoryOrigin has you covered with video tutorials. I also needed to upload all my book's metadata, including the title, subtitle, author name, book description, and book cover. Once I had all the content uploaded, I selected my preferred platform for my reviews.

The rest was up to me. I had to share it with my following and invite my email subscribers to join the ARC team. When people came into request access, I could accept or reject them based on their posts and their prior experience on various platforms. The nice part is StoryOrigin asks the reader for their Amazon reviewer profile so I could get an idea of their review history.

After my book launched, I sent a notification with an Amazon link for all of my ARC readers to leave a review. StoryOrigin makes life easy, and the best part is, it's completely affordable for all self-publishers.

I'd be remiss if I didn't mention one key area StoryOrigin has dialed in – newsletter swaps. You're able to collaborate with other authors in or around your genre through your email list. If you have a book or ARC you want to promote, you can have another author share it with their email newsletter. In return, you promote one of their products. The best part is you can see what the other author wants you to promote long before you agree to do the newsletter swap.

Newsletter swaps are a great way to work with other authors to raise brand awareness. You're able to cross-pollinate and grow your respective lists. If you lack content to send out to subscribers, then newsletter swaps are an easy way to provide continued value to your list. Just be selective about who you align with for this purpose. Always double-check their content and make sure it makes sense to promote it.

For instance, I have no issue with doing a newsletter swap, but you won't find me working with fiction authors for my nonfiction brand devoted to self-publishing. I can't justify the promotion, and it will confuse my subscribers. I don't want to erode the trust of my subscribers or irritate them with irrelevant offers. Also, I'm selective with how many swaps I do. I don't want to overwhelm myself with the extra work or turn off my readers because that's all I'm doing is promoting everyone else.

When building out your email list, growing your ARC team, and collaborating with other authors, remember why you're doing it in the first place – the reader. If you never lose sight of why you want to build an email list in the first place, you'll never go wrong. You should build an email list as a way to connect with your readers. If ever the day comes when you no longer use or require Amazon for your author brand, then at least you took your audience with you.

*A*dmittedly, I saved the best for last. It's a huge topic you shouldn't take lightly - networking. I believe networking is the most underutilized tool in marketing and promotion for books. Quite a few authors are known for being reclusive and introverted, hidden away from the world. The biggest problem lies therein. How can you even begin to expect people to find your books, much less, discover who you are if you're in some shack that's miles off the grid?

Ever hear the phrase:

> It's all about who you know.

That's not just some cheeky phrase or a line concocted by a crazed conspiracy theorist. It's the actual truth. The more people you know and have in your network, the more avenues open up to you as an author. The issues are:

1. Where do you begin?

2. Who do you talk to?

3. How does networking work?

4. How does it serve your author brand?

I was reluctant to break into this topic because a single chapter couldn't begin to cover what I learned through decades of experience in networking. I'll do my best to give you a few highlights and tips to get you started on the right foot. That way, you can build a network of business professionals on which you can rely.

Simply put, networking is when you create a group of acquaintances and associates. To keep your network active, you'll need to communicate regularly. It seems rather daunting at first, but it's much the same as writing an epic novel. It's never a good idea to write an 80,000-word or longer manuscript in one sitting. Instead, you should slowly chip away at crafting your book, one day at a time with one micro-step per movement. Building out your network isn't something that will happen overnight or through one business meeting. It takes plenty of interactions before you can lean on a business professional to be in your network.

Before you go to a Chamber of Commerce meeting or join a local meetup, you need to get a basic understanding of etiquette while networking. I've been to hundreds of meetings, and I can assure you, many business professionals get it wrong. The bad example is usually the blowhard, ego-centric entrepreneur who's there for the food while littering his business card everywhere. A good example is easier than you know. If you skip this chapter, then at least remember this little set of rules:

1. Ask questions.

2. Be approachable.

3. Try to make a new friend.

4. Listen more than you talk.

5. Offer your contact info only when asked.

133

These rules apply to all walks, whether you're doing in-person events or online virtual meetups. It requires no work whatsoever, and people will appreciate you for it.

People love to know when you hear them, so it's no surprise that people love to answer questions, especially when it's about them or their business. One of the easiest icebreakers for networking is just to introduce yourself and immediately ask their name. Follow it up by asking what they do for a living and for how long. That's enough to grease the wheels on the conversation. Don't stop asking questions. I challenge myself never to tell the other person my profession until they nearly demand to know what I do. Why? Again, people love to talk about themselves and their business. Since you already know what you're all about, what's the point in sharing it? So, you can hear it out loud? People truly don't care what you know until they know that you actually care.

Don't just ask questions to fill dead air. Show genuine interest in the other person. It might be a stretch at first, but everyone has common ground. If you ask enough questions, you'll find that common ground.

If you're an introvert like me, then it might be your first inclination to be a wallflower at networking events. That's okay as long as you don't wait until the last minute to act. The easiest way to warm up is to go directly to the first person you see and start a conversation. It sucks at first and sometimes feels incredibly awkward, but once you talk to one person, it's much easier to talk to others.

If you're not the type of person to start a conversation, at least remain approachable. That means you put your cellphone down for a minute. It's a crutch anyway. Open yourself up and make eye contact with other people. I promise it won't hurt to put on a smile. It doesn't need to be cheesy or over the top. Just give people a slight inclination that you won't bite if they approach you.

At social events, avoid hovering around the food or drinks table. You might as well be buried nose deep in your phone. Though the food is there for consumption, it can be a crutch and prevent you from chatting with everyone. I typically stuff my face full before I go to an event, so the only thing I need is a bottle of water when I arrive. The worst type of conversation is when you start chatting about the food or catering. Nope! The food isn't going to be a good common ground. After all, how do you pivot your conversation from the food to your author brand? It's near impossible.

When at business meetups, I try to make a new friend. There's nothing shady about my approach, and I have no ulterior motive. I want to find someone with whom I can connect. Not just on a business level, but on a personal level too. Do I count them out if we don't click on a visceral level? No, but it certainly helps to build a connection that's deeper and more meaningful beyond business.

The biggest mistake I see many people making at these types of meetings is talking too much. Don't get me wrong, you should talk, but know how to read the room. Share only enough to get the conversation going. If you find the conversation dying down, you can fire things back up with a thought-provoking question. When I recommend listening more than you talk, I don't insinuate you sit on your thumbs and wait your turn. You just have to find a balance between motormouth and wallflower.

The last rule I gave was to offer your contact info only when asked. Should you go to a business meeting with cards? Absolutely! Is it required? No. Because if you're making meaningful connections with other business professionals, then chances are likely, they won't need cardstock with your information on it. If you made enough of a good impression, they'll remember you and go searching for your contact.

One of my favorite things to do is go to a business meeting without a business card. Yes, I do it purposely. It forces me to be proactive in my conversations. The first thing I do when asked for a business card is to tell them I don't have any, but I have them pull out their phone and dial in my website, YouTube channel, or Amazon profile page. They'll most likely glance at it and continue the conversation. Later on, when they go into their phone, they will be reminded of me and our conversation. The nice part is it didn't cost me a dime and functioned better than any business card since it showed them my brand instead of some general contact info.

If you do have business cards, only take about half a dozen with you to meetings. That way, it forces you to be selective with who gets your card. There's nothing worse than leaving a meeting and seeing your cards littered all over the place. Mitigate this issue by handing out far less.

Speaking of business cards, what do you do with them? For me, I rarely hold onto a business card. It's clutter, and I have no use for them if I use a simple strategy. The day after a meeting, follow up with the person who handed you the business card. Send an email or call them. It doesn't need to be anything fancy and depends mostly on what you chatted about at your meeting. The simple act of follow-up is one that has left an indelible impression on my network. If I don't have a lot of time, I take a picture of the card and toss it out. I always include a follow-up sequence, so I stay in front-of-mind of my network.

I met a good friend, Melina Shah, at a local Chamber of Commerce meeting. We hit it off from the get-go and have kept loose contact with each other over the years. Melina used to use an app that scanned business cards. The app would store all the important data and then place the business professional into a contact sequence. She would get little reminders to reach out to the person. Also, Melina had someone in her contact list who would be of help when she needed it.

One of the things you should not do is enter a conversation with the sole intent of pushing your agenda. I used to work with a guy in network marketing who was the next level of creepy. This guy would go to grocery stores with zero intention of buying food. His only intent was to meet people and try to push his multi-level marketing (MLM) products on them. It was predatory and off-putting.

Do not get into networking if your sole intent is to push your agenda. When you show people you care, they'll become your biggest cheerleader, but when you show people you only care for yourself, you won't make many friends.

That's the whole thing around networking – building a network of friends and acquaintances you can lean on. That way, when it comes time for you to get help on your next launch, you can call on them. When you need help with a specific aspect of your business, you can call on someone. When you are stuck and don't know a way out, you can call on your network.

Where exactly do you find places to network? There's an unending supply of places to check out. Here are a few:

- Local meetups – Check your local Chamber of Commerce, Meetup.com, or local Facebook Groups.

- Social Media Outreach – Be tasteful and selective with how you approach people on social media. Don't be that weird guy spamming people's LinkedIn direct messages. Treat any virtual meeting like an in-person meeting. Follow the same rules as mentioned previously.

- **Online Virtual Meetings and Conferences** — Again, you can find these types of gatherings through Meetup.com or local Facebook Groups. Ask around, and you might find more.

- **In-Person Conferences** – This is, by far, the most beneficial of all the ways I network. When someone is willing to invest in an in-person conference, they're extremely motivated to elevate their business. Also, you have a common ground, so the ice-breaker conversation is way easier.

If you're feeling somewhat overwhelmed at the prospect of networking, it's okay. Everyone has been there. Don't let my little rules limit you. It's okay if you stumble because you can always dust yourself off and get back at it again. The most important thing to do when it comes to networking is – just do it. It's better you try than make no effort at all. You're only one contact away from extending your reach and exploding your author platform.

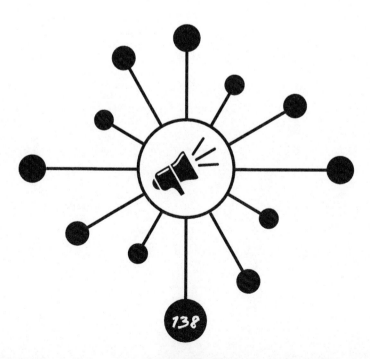

138

etting reviews for your book should be an integral part of your marketing and promotion plan. Though some would-be experts would have you believe getting a certain number of reviews is the trick to gaining the favor of Amazon, that isn't necessarily true. As shared in my book *Amazon Keywords for Books*, reviews play a small part in building relevance for your title in the Amazon algorithm. Still, the results are fleeting and don't last.

What does last is the impression a reader makes when posting a review of your book on the Amazon platform. It's the catchy buzzword people throw around called "social proof." Don't let the buzzword fool you; it's a fancy way of saying you got third-party credibility. By having a reader post their candid thoughts of your work, more potential readers can make an informed purchase when they come across your book on Amazon.

Can you sell books without having any reviews? Sure! I've sold hundreds of books with no reviews. Can you imagine how many more I would've sold had I gotten a few more people to post their honest insights?

Reviews reveal the experience the buyer had to the browsing customer. Whether perceived as good or bad, a review tells a story about your book. That story can be one that informs a potential reader about how they might enjoy your work. Remember, even when you get a low scoring review, those can also be beneficial to the growth of your book.

Book reviews are a great way to market your product on Amazon better. A book with more reviews appears more attractive than one that doesn't have any. Reviews also play an integral part in your promotion plan because you can share snippets of what readers enjoyed most about your work. Sometimes, a reader says it better than the writer. Rather than trying to come up with the best ad copy, a review snippet will suffice.

Instead of going neck-deep into another topic, I will put a pin in the book reviews topic for the third part in the *Amazon Self Publisher Series, Amazon Reviews for Books*. Getting book reviews is a challenging and often misunderstood part of the self-publishing process. For now, I recommend making review gathering a part of your marketing and promotion strategy. A little goes a long way!

*A*fter my mother left my eighteenth birthday celebration, I knocked on a few doors in my dorm. One person after the other came flocking to gobble down the free bits of leftover cake. Before I knew it, the whole cake was history. None of my newfound friends had any issue with staying and chatting. I came to form some early lifelong bonds with these relative strangers.

The following year, for my nineteenth birthday, I was already living off-campus. After having such a downer of a birthday party, I made sure to hype and promote the heck out of my party. My little two-bedroom apartment was full of people. We didn't eat just cake. Partygoers enjoyed oversized cookies, alcohol, pizza, and a wild assortment of goodies fit for an over-the-top celebration. The people who joined me included all my friends from the dorm. Not a single hometown acquaintance attended that night. Frankly, I didn't miss them. We were having too much fun to miss anyone.

Heck, the party got so loud, and out of hand, even the cops paid us a visit to quiet us down a little. That didn't put a damper on things, and the party continued to run off the rails. My previous birthday party paled in comparison. All it took was a little more hyping, building more relationships, and getting to know what my audience wanted from a party.

What a difference one year makes. I met many new people and made quite a few new friends. They were more than happy to show up. Some of them even came early and never left until the next morning!

That's how your book should be. When you put pen to paper, the world should already know about it. As you churn out chapter after chapter of content, people need to know your book is on its way. Once your book launches, your ideal reader should be feverishly waiting to snatch a copy out of your hands. After the book is out, remind readers often of it being there.

Once you finish having a book that only your mother can be proud of, let's get you to publish a book the whole world can enjoy too. Now, get out there and market your book right and promote it till kingdom come!

Now you finished reading this book, what did you think of what you read? Were there any tips or information you found insightful? What do you think was missing from this book? While you're thinking back on what you read, it'd mean the world to me if you left an honest review on Amazon.

As you probably know, reviews play a part in building relevancy for all products on Amazon. Whether you found the information helpful or not, your candid review would help other customers make an informed purchase.

Also, based on your review, I'll adjust this publication and future editions. That way, you and other indie authors can learn and grow.

Feel free to leave a review at DaleLinks.com/ReviewMPBook.

Dale L. Roberts is a self-publishing advocate, fitness author, and video content creator. Dale's inherent passion for life fuels his self-publishing advocacy both in print and online. After publishing over 40 titles and becoming a multiple international bestselling author on Amazon, Dale started his YouTube channel, Self-Publishing with Dale. Voted by Feedspot among the Top 100 websites and Top 50 YouTube channels devoted to self-publishing, Dale cemented his position as the go-to authority in the indie-author community.

Dale currently lives with his wife Kelli and cat Izzie in Columbus, Ohio.

Relevant links:

- Website – SelfPublishingWithDale.com

- YouTube – YouTube.com/SelfPublishingWithDale

- Twitter – Twitter.com/SelfPubWithDale

- Facebook – Facebook.com/SelfPubWithDale

- Instagram – Instagram.com/SelfPubWithDale

- DON'T GO HERE! – DaleLinks.com

Become a Keyword Master and Watch Your Book Sales Grow

If you can master keywords, then you can master your book's success! Dale L. Roberts is here to help you do that! In Amazon Keywords for Books, Dale shows you how to use keywords to sell more books. It's not difficult to increase the discoverability of your book. But you'll need a deeper understanding of keywords if you want to sell more books.

If you're ready to learn more and sell more through keyword mastery, then get your copy of Amazon Keywords for Books at...

DaleLinks.com/KeywordsBook

If all went well, it's only been about thirty to sixty days since I launched my last book *Amazon Keywords for Books*. I intended to rapidly release the *Amazon Self-Publishing* Series books to finally make this massive pivot from fitness author to self-publishing education. In this big move away from my old brand, I've run into some speed bumps along the way and had the help of quite a few friends.

Because it'd be absolutely insane for me to start with anyone else, the first person I have to thank for her undying love and support is my wife, Kelli. You are my biggest cheerleader and supporter through all of this. What people don't know is that you function as an integral part behind the scenes of *Self-Publishing with Dale*. You act as a sounding board, a consultant, and a therapist. Without Kelli, the *Self-Publishing with Dale* brand would be a hot mess.

Speaking of being a hot mess, I could not possibly even begin to accomplish half the things I do without the unwavering support of my ever-faithful assistant, Ava Fails. In my last manuscript, she spent a sleepless night editing my work. You can imagine my shock and surprise when I got my book back within twenty-four hours. I wish I could refer more people to Ava for business, but she is inundated with work. That's what makes working with her all the more special to me. If she didn't like working with me, she could've stopped a long time ago. It makes my day that Ava chooses to continue working with me. Thank you…and please, go easy on this manuscript.

Big thanks to Dan Norton, my video editor, for my renewed enthusiasm and direction with the *Self-Publishing with Dale* YouTube Channel. It's been awesome getting to know you beyond our shared love of wrestling. I appreciate how you pushed me outside my comfort zone to share with the world who I am beyond just some guy who obsessively talks about self-publishing. Where some followers have fallen off in the wake of my new direction, quite a few magnificent people replaced them. This is all due to Dan believing in me and my message. You're the best, man!

Rob Archangel is a saint, and I'll fight you if you disagree with me. When I was ready to format the manuscript for *Amazon Keywords for Books*, I reached out to Rob about his services in Archangel Ink. Out of the kindness of his heart, he agreed to work with me. His patience makes even Job himself blush. I had many demands and required a ton of attention to get my manuscript looking just right. As part of my thank you to Rob, I'm asking you, the reader, to take a moment to browse Archangel Ink's services when you visit ArchangelInk.com. Tell them Dale sent you!

If you listen closely, you'll hear the gigantic avalanche of names I'm about to drop for all their love and support, including the folks in the self-publishing community: Keith Wheeler, Kevin Maguire, Mojo Siedlak, Julie Broad, Dave Chesson, Michael La Ronn, Catrina Taylor, Andrew Wong, Jonel Fernando, Bonnie Phillips, Sylvia Hubbard, Lee Jones, Saketh Kumar, Jacob Rothenberg, Orna Ross & the Alliance of Independent Authors.

Of course, a big thanks to all my video content creator friends: Dan Currier, Jason Stallworth, Terrance from Inside the Lab PC Tech,

Nick Nimmin, Dee Nimmin, Brian G Johnson TV, Roberto Blake, Derral Eves, and more.

If I happened to miss your name, I apologize. As you can imagine, it's hard for me to recall every last person who has been responsible for my growth and success. If I missed your name, please reach out to me, and I'll resolve that issue in future releases. Know that I appreciate your love and support and do not take it lightly.

Lastly, you, the reader! I appreciate you parting ways with your time, energy, attention, and money to read this book. It means the world to me, and I hope you found some value and inspiration to move your author brand in the right direction. Thank you from the bottom of my heart.

- Archangel Ink – DaleLinks.com/ArchangelInk
- Advanced Reader Copy hosting
  - Storyorigin – StoryOrig.in
  - Fiveabook – Fiveabook.com
  - NOTE: Both websites are in open beta and may switch to a premium model at any time. Get access while they're still free!
- Background removal by Fiverr – DaleLinks.com/Kaysar
- Book Brush – for free and premium graphic assets – think Canva for authors on steroids –BookBrush.com.
- Books about Amazon Ads
  - Brian Meeks – *Mastering Amazon Ads*
  - Chris Fox – *Ads for Authors Who Don't Like Math*
- Books about email marketing
  - *Invisible Selling Machine* by Ryan Deiss
  - *Dotcom Secrets* by Russel Brunson
- Captioning services by Rev – DaleLinks.com/Rev.
- Free image resources:
  - Pixabay - Pixabay.com
  - Vecteezy - Vecteezy.com

- > Pexels - Pexels.com/
- > Visual Hunt - Visualhunt.com/
- > Unsplash - Unsplash.com/
- > Gratisography - Gratisography.com
- > Freepik - Freepik.com
- > New Old Stock - Nos.twnsnd.co
- > Stock Snap - Stocksnap.io
- > Flickr - Flickr.com/creativecommons
- > Free Images - Freeimages.com
- > Wikimedia - Commons.wikimedia.org/wiki/Main_Page
- Image background removal – Remove.bg at DaleLinks.com/RemoveBG
- Jason Jones publicist – DaleLinks.com/PRToolkit
- Publisher Rocket – DaleLinks.com/Rocket
- Social media automation by ContentStudio – DaleLinks.com/ContentStudio
- YouTube experts I trust & follow
  - > Nick Nimmin - YouTube.com/NickNimmin
  - > Brian G Johnson - YouTube.com/BrianGJohnsonTV
    - * Tube Ritual on FB - Facebook.com/groups/TubeRitual
  - > Roberto Blake - YouTube.com/RobertoBlakePSD
  - > Derral Eves - YouTube.com/DerralEves

1   Clement, J. (10 August 2020). Number of monthly active Facebook users worldwide as of 2nd quarter 2020. https://www.statista.com/statistics/264810/number-of-monthly-active-facebook-users-worldwide/.

2   IEEE Communications Society. (10 June 2017). Cisco: Online video to account for 82% of all Internet traffic by 2021! https://techblog.comsoc.org/2017/06/10/cisco-increased-use-of-web-video-to-be-82-of-all-internet-traffic-by-2021/.

3   Hubspot, Inc. (25 September 2018). The Top 7 Search Engines, Ranked by Popularity. https://blog.hubspot.com/marketing/top-search-engines.

4   D'Anastasio, C. (22 June 2020). Microsoft Gives Up on Mixer. https://www.wired.com/story/microsoft-shutting-down-mixer-facebook-gaming/.

5   Kim, E. (25 August 2014). Amazon Buys Twitch For $970 Million In Cash. https://www.businessinsider.com/amazon-buys-twitch-2014-8.

6   Schultz, M. (n.d.). How Many Touches Does It Take to Make a Sale? https://www.rainsalestraining.com/blog/how-many-touches-does-it-take-to-make-a-sale.

Printed in Great Britain
by Amazon